Chartres

Chartres
AND THE BIRTH OF THE CATHEDRAL

BY

TITUS BURCKHARDT

Translated from the German by William Stoddart

Foreword by Keith Critchlow

WORLD WISDOM BOOKS

First published in German by Urs Graf Verlag 1962
Chartres und die Geburt der Kathedrale

Library of Congress Cataloging-in-Publication Data
Burckhardt, Titus.
[Chartres und die Geburt der Kathedrale. English]
Chartres and the birth of the cathedral / by Titus Burckhardt
translated from the German by William Stoddart; foreword by Keith Critchlow.
p. cm.
Includes bibliographical references and index.
ISBN 0-941532-21-6 (alk. paper)
ISBN 0-941532-23-2 (cased)
1. Cathédrale de Chartres. 2. Architecture, Gothic—France—Chartres. 3. Chartres (France)—Buildings, structures, etc.
I. Title.
na5551.c5b8613 1996 726'.6'094451—dc20 95-32639

Typeset by Goodfellow & Egan, Cambridge, England
Printed by A. G. Elkar, S. Coop. Bilbao. Spain

Cover photo of Chartres Cathedral
by permission of Sonia Halliday & Laura Lushington

The titlepage illustration depicts the Holy Virgin
in the flowering tree of Jesse. Drawing from the Jesse window
of Chartres Cathedral by J. B. A. Lassus.

United States of America publication by
World Wisdom Books, Inc.
P.O. Box 2682, Bloomington, Indiana 47402-2682

Contents

Foreword

THIS book may well turn out to be the most important of its kind written in this century. However, it is necessary to say on what basis one comes to such a conclusion after reading this exceptional work.

Titus Burckhardt's text fulfils its historical mission of reintroducing to the contemporary mentality the essential reasons for the creation of this cathedral and the depth of understanding that underlay it, in a manner not so far attempted by any author this century, notwithstanding the brilliant scholarship of Otto von Simpson's *The Gothic Cathedral* and the sensitive spiritual exploration of René Querido's *The Golden Age of Chartres*. Here we have evidence of a profound understanding by Burckhardt that nothing less than a four-fold explanation – such as was taught at the School of Chartres itself – is called for.

So much so that we can say the achievement contained in these pages is the expression of an inspiration that could only come from the principial Unity itself. Burckhardt explains the four-fold 'levels' or aspects with a characteristic brilliance of scholarship appropriately serving the same ideals as the subject he is writing about. These levels are properly understood by the receptive soul as degrees of symbolic transparency corresponding to levels of intellectual-contemplative states of being. The following extract describes these depths of meaning; '... the medieval exegetes, following an ancient tradition, maintained every image in Holy Scripture can be interpreted in several senses. William Durandus writes that in Holy Scripture, there are four principal meanings: historical, allegorical, tropological and anagogical'. Durandus explains this as follows: 'Historically, Jerusalem is the city in Palestine to which people went on pilgrimage; allegorically (or morally), it is the Church Militant; tropologically, it is the Christian soul; and analogically, it is the Heavenly Jerusalem, the eternal home.' Thus, above and beyond the historical, the allegorical indicates the parallel meanings of a moral imperative that unites the separate interpretations; the tropological indicates the metaphorical or figurative – 'turning the soul', from the original Greek *tropos* = turning; the anagogical being the summation of knowledge, the spiritual meaning which unifies all other levels into a profound unity, from the Greek *anagogos* to 'lead up'.

It may seem unnecessary to dwell on this aspect of Burckhardt's presentation, but it does establish the important depth of significance for a contemporary milieu where meaning in architecture has been whittled down exclusively to the so-called 'functional'; relating merely to the mechanical-material working level. The question of function has been addressed by Burckhardt here in the most responsible way, that is combining scholarship with spiritual insight. Here we have an author who refuses to evaluate so unique a building as Chartres in contemporary (psychological) terms. And this explains the author's warning in the opening words of the book against reading the text as art history, as this would limit the subject to the historicist's perspective, thus, in effect, banishing it to the archives of the past. Chartres is a living reality to those who visit it – as much today as when it was completed.

One cannot but be reminded of the words Christopher Wren had engraved on his modest tomb in the crypt of St Paul's cathedral in London: 'If you want to know about Christopher Wren look about you'. The purpose of this study is clearly stated: '... to evoke as authentically as possible, the spiritual climate in which the Gothic Cathedral was born'. To strengthen his avowed purpose Burckhardt displays an incisive scholarship in quoting contemporary witnesses themselves – not just for historical ends, but to demonstrate that such witness works integrally with the four levels of function as we might describe them: the historical (political and social) function of the Church; the ethical, practical function of *how* things were accomplished; the cultural, intellectual and objective function of establishing the priciples of beauty; and the final, all embracing inspirational function or spiritual unity that the building represents: in short a profound and simple unicity. This would be impossible without a knowledge of the Christian doctrines in the first place, allied to the objectivity of the Platonic philosophy that in turn renders intelligible the mysterious functions of a knowledge that is by its nature beyond the scope of the rational discursive mind. Burckhardt clearly demonstrates the extensive use made by the School of Chartres of the intellectual-contemplative 'support' of the Quadrivium of number as *arithmetic*, number, or space as *geometry*, number in time as *music* or harmony and number in space and time as *astronomy*.

Nowhere in Christendom has there been a more successful marriage of the objective knowledge of the Platonic corpus with the metaphysical import of the Christian revelation than at Chartres. Firstly, in the School itself through such luminaries as Fulbert and Bernard Silvestris, Gilbert de la Porée, the great Thierry, as well as our own English abbot at Chartres, John of Salisbury. And secondly, as a result of the School's teaching in support of the Christian revelation by means of the substance that is the edifice of the finest of the proto-cathedrals – Chartres.

Not only is this book a feast to the hungers of the soul, but it cannot fail to inspire the sensitive reader to become a pilgrim to the noble sanctuary itself.

Keith Critchlow
London, March 1995

Preface

THE purpose of the present work is to evoke as authentically as possible the spiritual climate in which the Gothic cathedral was born, and to do so by allowing contemporary witnesses to speak for themselves—rather in the manner of my earlier book *Siena, City of the Virgin.*[1] My aim here is to show how the Gothic cathedral was the final fruit to ripen on the tree of an ancient tradition. Since Chartres cathedral was the first 'classical' cathedral in the Gothic style, I have made it the object of my study.

From the standpoint of the agitated and over-cerebral age in which we live, medieval men often seem naïve, child-like, and untouched by psychological uncertainty, and this can mislead us into thinking that they were less reflective and more instinctive than ourselves. In reality, however, their actions were inspired by a vision or an idea—namely, the spiritual meaning of life—to a much greater extent than in the case of modern man. It was precisely because they lived for a timeless truth that their love and their creative joy gave rise to that undivided strength which we see and admire in their productions. As has been said, they were closer both to Heaven and to earth than are we.

In modern man, generally speaking, it is the exact opposite: his motivation is chiefly sentiment, in the service of which a whole apparatus of mental activity, theories and 'ideologies' is brought into play. On the surface, the operation of mind and brain is highly visible, but underneath the motivating factor is individual or collective passion. To put it another way: in traditional artists, it is the element 'object' that determines the work, whereas in most modern artists, it is the element 'subject'.

To understand modern man, it may well be appropriate to study psychology; but one can only understand medieval man if one is aware of his highest aims and aspirations, and if one perceives how and to what extent his ideas symbolically express that which is universally and eternally true.

☾

I have described the fundamental principles of sacred art in my book *Sacred Art in East and West.*[2] In the present volume, these principles were confirmed and amplified by the primary sources consulted and also by *The Gothic Cathedral* by Otto von Simson and *Die Entstehung der Kathedrale* by Hans Sedlmayr. Important insights were also obtained from *L'art religieux du XIIe et XIIIe siècles en France* by Emile Mâle and *Europäische Kunstgeschichte* by Peter Meyer.

The Earliest Models

WHEN we hear the word 'cathedral', we think immediately of the large ecclesiastical buildings of the twelfth and thirteenth centuries, with which the Gothic style reached its zenith. All these churches were indeed built as bishops' seats, that is to say as cathedrals in the literal sense of the word. Strictly speaking, however, the first of all Latin cathedrals is St. Peter's in Rome, for it contains the late-Roman *sedia gestatoria* which, as the *cathedra Petri*, the chair or seat of the Prince of the Apostles, is the prototype and model of all subsequent episcopal thrones. At the time of the construction of the first Gothic cathedrals, this ancient chair—which, with the building of the new St. Peter's, was enclosed in Bernini's gigantic marble throne—still stood in the apse of the original basilica, which was built by Constantine and subsequently underwent little change.

The *sedia gestatoria* said to have been used as his 'chair' (*cathedra*) by the Apostle Peter. The back, consisting of columns, was added in the early Middle Ages. (Taken from Schüller-Pirolli, *2000 Jahre Sankt Peter*, Olten, Switzerland, 1950)

This served as the model for church building in the Christian West, not so much in its detail as in its general disposition, which was a well-thought out liturgical plan, of whose antecedents we know little; quite simply, it was suddenly there, with the earliest churches, and since then it served as a standard. And yet the form of the original St. Peter's, as we know it from early sketches, so much resembled the official buildings of imperial Rome, with their classical rows of pillars under horizontal archivolts, that it strikes us as almost pagan, and certainly

View into the nave and two pairs of aisles of the original St. Peter's Basilica (from Schüller-Pirolli, *op. cit.*)

not yet fully Christian. This is partly explained by the fact that Christian art, and especially architecture, had not yet had time to find its own language; there is also a positive reason for this impression, in that the architecture of these Roman basilicas—which in name were 'royal' buildings, but in fact were 'city' buildings—was consciously taken over by the Christians: for the Church was the reflection of the City of God. Just as St. Augustine, in his famous work, had likened the City of God, the 'Heavenly Jerusalem', to the earthly city (of which the city of Rome, the *civitas*, was the model), so early Christian architecture also based itself on the model of the city, as represented by the imperial council chamber. Ecclesiastical architecture could not properly base itself on the pre-Christian Roman temple, if only because this was not intended to house a congregation; its purpose was to serve as the dwelling-place of a god; and there were many gods. Only the imperial civic model was appropriate, and this the now victorious—but previously illegal—Christianity sought to adapt spiritually, at the risk of bringing into its own camp the old opposition between the earthly and the heavenly 'city'.

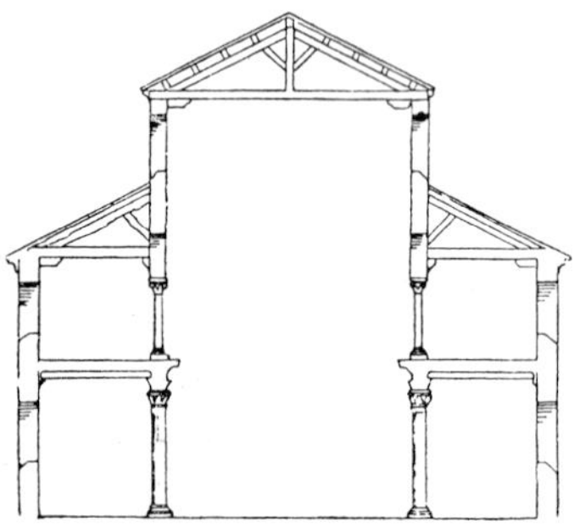

Cross-section of a Roman basilica with raised galleries.

In its form, a basilica may be compared to a covered street, with a clerestory and side arcades. In fact the basilicas in the heart of Roman cities were like streets converted into large halls. Sometimes the aisles (flanking the nave) had raised galleries, in which case these corresponded to the upper stories of the houses rising on either side of the street. To this day, arcaded streets are typical of city centres in Latin countries.[3]

The old St. Peter's basilica had no raised choir, so that the walls, which extended beyond the two rows of pillars of the central nave to the top of the lean-to roofs on either side, provided large surfaces for mosaics and, above these, sufficient room for windows. If, in one's imagination, one traces this type of building back to its most primitive form, to the image of a large hall supported by wooden pillars (that is to say, tree trunks stripped of their bark), and obtaining light from the fact that its central 'nave' rises higher than its lateral 'aisles' and is open-sided in its higher reaches, we arrive at a prototype as simple as it is perfect. This prototype was easily realized in wood, but only relatively late, namely in the earliest Gothic pillar architecture (and first of all in Chartres), did it find such an easy and luminous expression in stone.

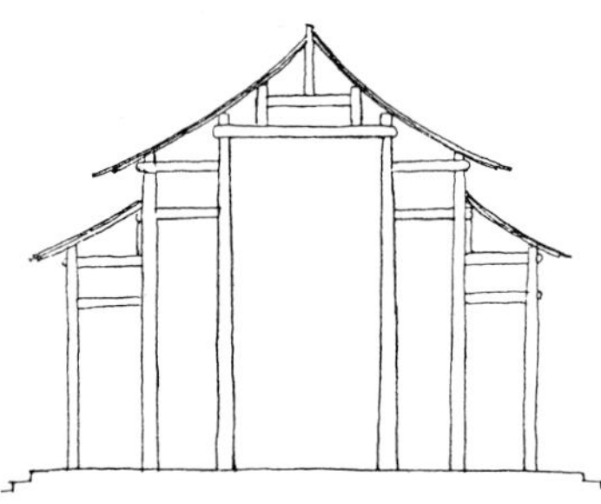

Cross-section of an early Japanese pillared edifice in wood, with 'nave' and two pairs of 'aisles'.

Basilican pillar construction was already used in ancient Egyptian temples. The early Christian basilica shares with them the fact that it is both a longitudinal passage-way and a sanctuary. Its similarity to a street leading towards a destination is clearly visible when one looks at the overall lay-out of a church like the old St. Peter's. There was the forecourt or atrium, located in front of the long nave and aisles, which served as a transition between the outside world and the sanctuary.

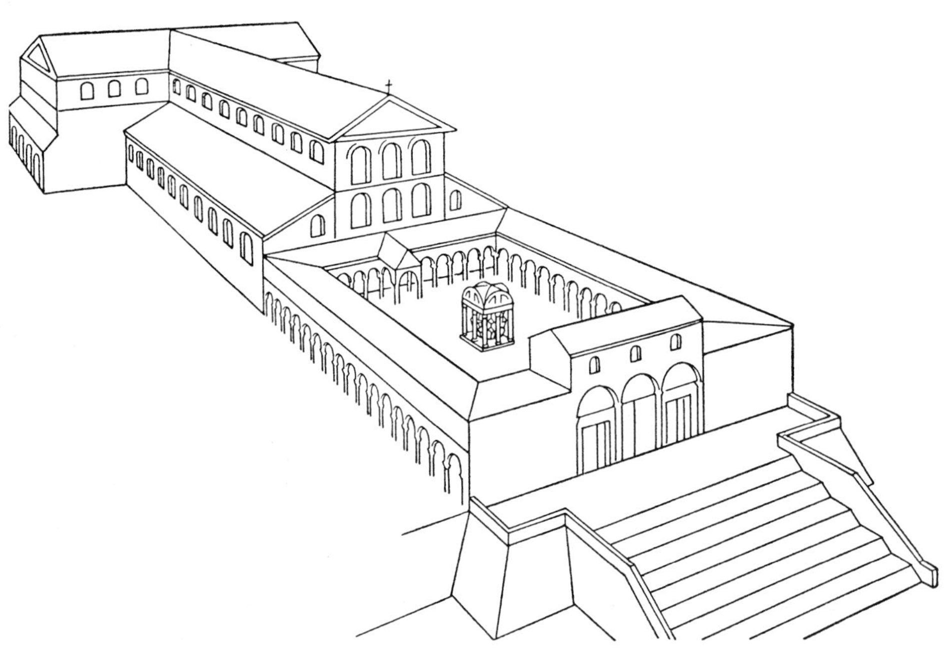

Artist's reconstruction of the Constantinian Basilica of St. Peter.

The forecourt was surrounded by colonnades and was originally planted with all kinds of decorative plants such as cypresses, laurels and roses, which made it an image of the earthly paradise, after which it was also named. In the centre stood the famous *pigna* fountain, a gigantic bronze pine-cone from out of which jets of water gushed into a basin of porphyry. The basin was decorated with griffins. Above it rose a marble baldachin which had pairs of peacocks on its gables and jumping dolphins on its eaves. Perhaps this fountain was taken from a pre-Christian building, and yet its symbols, which seem to originate in Asia rather than in the Greco-Roman world, were already well assimilated into the Christian perspective. They are also to be found in catacombs, early Christian sarcophagi and mosaics. As in ancient Mesopotamia, the pine-cone represents the evergreen tree from which the water of life flows. The fountain of life, according to legend, springs forth from the deepest place in the earth, the root of the world-tree, where dwells the peacock, adorned with a thousand starry eyes, and bearing the wheel of heaven. In the early Asiatic zodiac, the peacock must have represented the lowest house of heaven, in which the sun, turning from its setting to its rising movement, undergoes death and re-birth.[4] For Christians, the sun, the 'light that shineth in the darkness', was Christ. The griffin also referred to Him: a solar animal with a dual nature derived from the eagle and the lion. The dolphin also referred to Christ, the sacred fish which from ancient times had been linked with the solstice and its spiritual meaning: just as the dolphin jumps out of the dark sea to meet the light of day, so also the sun, after seeming, at its lowest point, to have risked drowning in the world-sea, rises in mid-winter to its new ascent.

The *pigna* (pine-cone) fountain, after drawings of the fifteenth and sixteenth centuries.

All of these images refer to spiritual rebirth and thus to baptism, through which the innocence of the earthly paradise may, depending on circumstances, be regained. In keeping with this, it was in the forecourt that the as yet unbaptized catechumens remained during the celebration of mass. It is probable that, before the baptistry was constructed, baptisms were carried out under the portico to the actual church.

From the forecourt one entered the large church, with its central nave and two pairs of aisles, which led towards the transept but which were separated from it by a prominent 'triumphal arch'. In the transept, in front of the apse and on a raised platform above the grave of the Apostle, stood the altar. A screen with spiral pillars and decorated with stylized vine branches separated both grave and altar from the nave.

The transept, which marked the end of the street-like nave—rather as the horizontal crossbar at the top of the letter T marks the end of the vertical line—was shut off by curtains that extended across the full width of the nave. Widened only slightly by the apse, the transept thus presented itself to the worshipper as the real sanctuary.

Forecourt, nave and transept corresponded respectively to the three stages of the Christian way spoken of by the Fathers of the Church, namely purification, illumination, and union with God. The first of these is represented by baptism, the second by spiritual instruction, and the third by the eucharist.

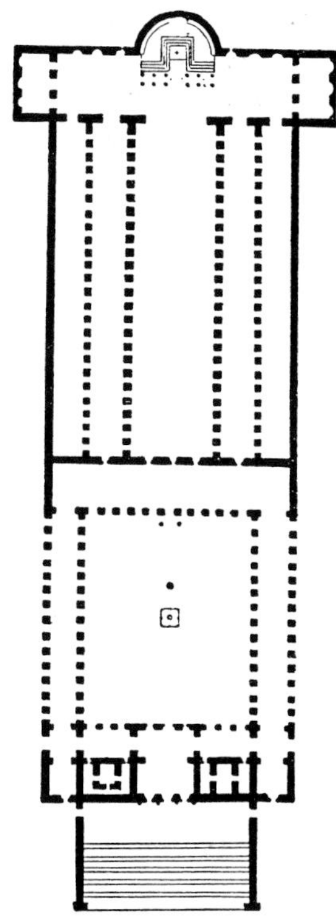

Groundplan of the Constantinian Basilica of St. Peter.

The apse, in which the bishop, as vicar of Christ and successor to Peter, had his throne, corresponded to Heaven, and this was symbolized not only by its vaulted form, but also by its pictorial decoration: in the half-cupola of the apse was a representation of Christ in Majesty. Already in pre-Christian places of worship, such as Mithraist temples, the vaulted niche signified Heaven, and although, as *exedra* (debating chamber) in the later period of pagan Rome, it was used for the display of official authority, its original meaning as a place of divine manifestation had never been completely forgotten and this was taken up anew by ecclesiastical architecture.

The builders of Constantine's basilica had all the more reason for wishing clearly to differentiate the successive stages (from forecourt to holy of holies), in that the church was now for the first time open and accessible to all, and its mysteries had to be protected from the general public. For this reason the altar was also surrounded by screens and surmounted by a ciborium or canopy, around which curtains could be drawn.

On the other hand, the Church, by its very nature, is a way that leads from the world to God, from earth to Heaven, and this is so because of her union with Christ, who declared that He Himself was the Way. In this respect, as a divinely founded way destined for all, she also stood in opposition to those schools of Greco-Roman philosophy which sought, through meditation and self-imposed *ascesis* alone, to reach a knowledge of God. The answer to them was given by St. Augustine as follows:

> It is a great and very rare thing for a man, after he has contemplated the whole of creation, corporeal and incorporeal, and has discerned its mutability, to pass beyond it and, by the continued soaring of his mind, to attain to the unchangeable being of God and, in that height of contemplation, to learn from God Himself that none but He has made all that is not of the divine nature. For God speaks with man not by means of some audible creature dinning in his ears... nor even by means of subtle images such as we see in dreams and similar states ... but by the truth itself... for He speaks to that part of man which is better than all else that is in him, and than which only God Himself is better.

For there is in man by nature something which can link him with God, namely the contemplative Intellect that is free from all subjectivism.

> But since the Intellect itself, though capable by nature of reason and intuition, has been weakened and obscured by deep-rooted vices, then, in order to enjoy—and even merely to tolerate—the unchangeable divine light, it must firstly be strengthened and purified by faith, so that it is gradually healed, renewed and made capable of such felicity. And so that the intellect might more confidently follow this way of faith towards the truth, the truth itself, God, God's son, assumed humanity—without shedding His divinity—and established the faith, thus enabling man to reach the God of man through the God-Man. He is the Mediator between God and men, the man Christ Jesus; inasmuch as He is man, He is the Mediator and the Way. For if there is a way that will lead the striver towards a goal that is striven after, the striver has hope of reaching it; but if there is no way, or if the striver knows not where the way is, of what use is it to know the goal? The only Way that is infallibly secured against all errors is He who is both God and man; as God He is the Goal, as man He is the Way. (*The City of God*, XI: 2)

The church—or the soul—as a 'ship' (nave); a mural from the Roman catacombs.

The choir of the old St. Peter's, like that of the present building, was directed towards the west. This positioning, which seems to infringe the customary rule, is explained by the fact that the priest, when celebrating mass, approached the altar from the choir side, and thus turned his face towards the east and towards the congregation. As is still the case today, the altar was situated directly above the tomb of St. Peter, the encasement of which rose above the floor level of the church and was opened towards the nave by means of a window.

The fact that the forecourt or 'paradise' was on the east side of the building is in accordance with the position ascribed to the earthly paradise by the Bible and from this one may conclude that the apse, located at the other end of the 'way' and decorated with the image of the universal Judge, is intended to symbolize the end of time.

If however the west corresponds to the end of the world, then, at the Last Judgement, the appearance of God arises, like the sun, in the east, and on this symbolism almost all later churches are founded, in that, with the choir, they face the east, so that both priest and people pray in the same direction. In connection with this, the bishop's throne is also moved back from out of the depth of the choir to the side of the altar, while the altar itself begins gradually to move towards the position once occupied by the throne. This exchange, which did not take place in exactly the same way in all places (and which in many places did not take place at all), was symbolically anticipated by the fact that the altar itself was regarded as the throne of God; from the time of the Ravenna mosaics to that of later icon painting, the 'prepared throne' and the altar were interchangeable images. In fact the altar, on which the transubstantiation occurs, is something like a seat of the divine presence: *sedes et corporis et sanguinis Christi*.

According to St. Basil and other Church Fathers, the custom of turning towards the east when praying goes back to apostolic times. The early Christians saw in the sun, which on Easter morning rises precisely in the east, the natural image of the Saviour who had risen from death to life. 'The house of the believers', according to what is written in the approximately 400 Apostolic Constitutions, 'is long in shape like a ship (nave) and directed towards the east'. The later liturgists added that the place of the equinox should be used as an orientation guide.

Since the nave runs from west to east, it follows that the transept lies in a north-south direction; the axial cross of the building thus corresponds to the axial cross of the heavens, and in this regard ecclesiastical architecture continues an ancient custom that reaches back to the origins of all architecture. Christian architecture may have taken this over from the craft lore of the builders of ancient Rome; for not only Roman temples, but also towns, streets, and parish boundaries, were wherever possible oriented according to the cosmic cross. Proof of this is that the whole visible order of the Roman *civitas* conformed to a celestial model. For the ancient Roman builders, members of the *collegia fabrorum*, the orientation of a building according to the directions of heaven certainly signified much more than a mere constructional aid. It was carried out in imitation of the order-giving act, through which the sun-god transformed chaos into cosmos; that is to say, it was a rite in the true sense of the term. Christianity, however, gave this rite a new meaning, which one can already perceive in the inscriptions of the catacombs, where a cross surrounded by a circle became the symbol of Christ. Sometimes, by the addition of the Greek letter *Chi* (i.e. X, which is the initial letter of *Christos*), it is extended to an eight-spoked universal wheel, and sometimes the first three letters of the Greek *Christos*, namely *Chi-Rho-Iota* (i.e. X-P-I, or, in Roman letters, Ch-R-I) form a six-spoked wheel, whose spokes correspond to the four directions of heaven together with the polar axis, a device which decorated the *labarum* (imperial standard) of the emperor Constantine. The symbol of the 'invincible sun' (*sol*

Byzantine monogram of the Name of Christ.

Monogram of the Name of Christ from the catacombs, composed of the Greek letters *chi* (X) and *rho* (P) in the form of a cross.

Monogram of the Name of Christ from the catacombs in the form of an eight-spoked wheel. Written between the spokes are the words: *In Christo bibas (vivas)* – 'Live in Christ!'.

invictus) that was accorded to the Roman emperor as ruler of the universal empire, was thus transmuted into the Name of Christ, the Divine Sun of the universe: *Orietur sicut sol Salvator mundi* ('The Saviour of the world shall arise like the sun'. Vigil of Christmas, *Malachi*, IV:2). And also: *Christus, lumen et splendor Patris, mundi salus, currens per anni circulum* ('Christ, Light and Splendour of the Father, salvation of the world, transcoursing the annual cycle'. *Hymnus in Vesperis Nativitatis*).

The custom of orienting a church building according to the directions of heaven is the logical counterpart to the time-reckoning by means of which the cycle of church feasts was assimilated to the Roman solar year. It must not be forgotten that for the people of antiquity and the Middle Ages, the divisions of time were inseparably linked with the divisions of space, as indeed they still are. For the basic measure of time remains the movement of the heavenly bodies, which itself can only be measured by the immutable standards constituted by the poles and solstices of the solar cycle. We of today have to remind ourselves of the reciprocal relationship of time and space; but for the ancients, who did not yet measure time by such a thing as the mechanical ticking of a clock, this was self-evident; and, because they regarded neither time nor space in a purely quantitative manner, time revealed itself to them as a rhythm, whose individual phases possessed a variety of properties, like so many high notes, while universal space was both physically and spiritually evaluated according to the directions of heaven which radiate immutably within it.

Liturgy also had recourse to the spiritual meaning of the various directions of heaven, and from the liturgy this spiritual meaning was transposed back to church architecture and to the distribution of images within it. The Gothic style developed this cosmic plan on the transparent walls of the cathedrals: thus, in Chartres cathedral, the pictorial windows in the east, where the sun rises, portray the incarnation of the eternal Word, the birth and the childhood of Christ, and in the west, where the sun sets, the Last Judgement. The north, however, is not merely regarded as the place of infernal darkness, but as the heavenly region where the sun travels unseen, before it rises over the horizon. For this reason, in Chartres, the pictures of the Old Covenant are to be found here.

☾

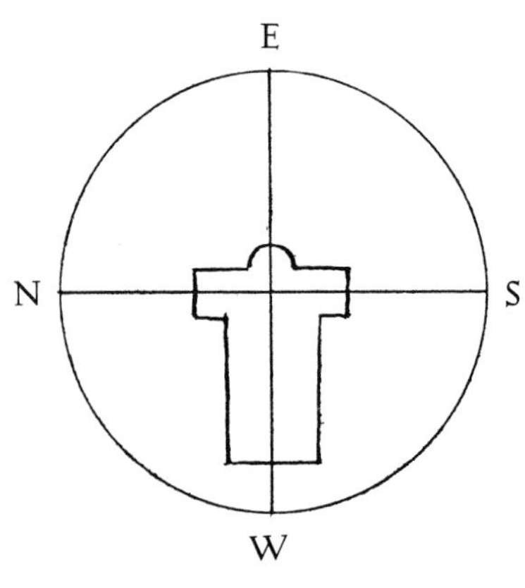

By the process of orientation, the sacred building is placed in the centre of the visible universe, for in it the main axes of the heavens intersect. Of course, space, in its immeasurable extension, has its centre everywhere; from every spot on earth the directions aiming at the fixed points in the heavenly vault reach out in the same way; but sacred architecture gives this ubiquity of the spatial centre its spiritual meaning, in that it firmly recalls that the true centre of the world is here, where God Himself is present, in the sacrifice of the altar, and in the heart of the worshipper.

If a medieval church building, a Romanesque minster, for example, appears as a cosmos resting in itself, this results from the fact that it incorporates in itself a vision of the universe that captures the physical spiritually and the spiritual physically. What the Romanesque and Gothic styles of architecture express in stone – a consciousness of the spiritual realities that surround man on all sides – Dante, at the end of the High Middle Ages, and as if to serve as its legacy, expressed in words. For the truth that the order of the visible universe extends far beyond itself, there is no better image than the concentric heavenly layers rising hierarchically from the lowest heaven, in which the moon moves round the earth, beyond all planetary orbits, up to the measureless vault of the fixed stars surrounded in its turn by the outermost and invisibly moving heaven, which itself rests in the Infinite. The angels are likewise ranked hierarchically, as are the stages of spiritual knowledge, extending from the temporal to the Eternal.

If one could have told an intelligent man of the Middle Ages that in reality space was quite different from what he imagined it to be – that the earth was not its centre and that the sun was not the largest heavenly body within it – his response would probably have been as follows: The universe certainly contains many things that we have not yet seen, and very many more that we never shall see, for our eyes are those of a human being, not those of an angel or a demon. Since, however, God has placed us in a setting wherein the earth on which we stand appears as *terra firma*, and the luminaries in the heavens appear to revolve around us in ever-increasing orbits, this must have a providential meaning for us.

The most general meaning of a sanctuary is the reconciliation of earth and Heaven. Therefore it is also a *sacratum*, a place set apart from every other earthly condition, for in it the otherwise prevailing separation of Heaven and earth, the fall of man and his world from the Eternal, are symbolically and spiritually overcome. In the architectural form of the sanctuary, this can be represented outwardly in several ways; however, the linking of the two existential poles 'heaven' and 'earth' is expressed with particular eloquence when the sanctuary consists of a square building surmounted by a cupola: the cupola represents heaven, whereas the earth, in its inert condition, subject to the four elements, the four natural qualities, and the four seasons, is 'square'.

The symbolism of this architectural form is so convincing that it was not possible that it should have remained foreign to Christian art. Probably its model came from Asia. That in Christian culture also it was understood as the symbol of the universe, is proved by a Syrian hymn[5] about the cathedral of Edessa, which was built in the sixth century, and, like its sister, the church of Hagia Sophia in Constantinople, was dedicated to Holy Wisdom. Edessa, now called Urfa, in north-western Mesopotamia, was then one of the greatest metropolitan cities of Christendom and its church was renowned in that it contained the *acheiropoietos* ('not-made-by-human-hand') icon of Christ, the miraculous copy of the Holy Face on a cloth, which, according to legend, Christ Himself gave to the ambassador of King Abgar of Edessa. Since the cathedral lay between two lakes, it seemed to be surrounded by water.

> Wonderful it is that this building in its smallness resembles the wide world, not through its size, but in its character: water surrounds it, just as the ocean surrounds the world; its roof is wide like heaven, without pillars, vaulted and everywhere closed, and decorated with golden mosaics as is the firmament with shining stars.
>
> Its noble cupola resembles the heaven of heavens. The upper part of the building rests on the lower part like a helmet.
>
> Its wide and splendid arches represent the four sides of the world. Through their multiplicity, its colours recall magnificent rainbows.
>
> Other arches surround it, like overhanging cliffs in the mountains. On them, in them, and through them, the cupola is attached to the four sides . . . .

It is likely that the cupola was supported at the four corners of its square base

by squinches, which like funnels became narrower as they descended and which, projecting laterally, propped up the large arches surmounting the square base.

> The marble of the church is like the not-by-human-hand-created icon. With this marble, the walls are harmoniously covered. By means of its bright surface it gathers within itself, like the sun, all light.
>
> The church is surrounded by magnificent forecourts and two pillared halls, which represent the twelve tribes of Israel, ranged around the tabernacle of the covenant.
>
> On three sides the building has the same face, just as the Holy Trinity repeats the same prototype three times.

In fact the building had three plain sides, and on the fourth side, the one facing east, there was an apse.

> In the choir, a rare light shines through three open windows: it announces the mystery of the Trinity of Father, Son, and Holy Spirit.
>
> The *ambo* (pulpit) is placed in the centre, following the prototype of the Last Supper in Zion. Eleven pillars stand upon it, like the eleven apostles who hid themselves at the place of the Last Supper.
>
> Another pillar, to the rear, recalls Golgotha. On it rises a shining cross like our Lord between the two thieves.
>
> Five doors open into the church, like the five wise virgins of the parable. The faithful gloriously enter through them like the virtuous host.
>
> The ten pillars which bear the cherub of the choir represent the ten apostles who were filled with horror when our Saviour was crucified.
>
> The nine steps leading up to the throne in the choir represent the nine ranks of angels who are crowned from the throne of Christ....

According to St. Dionysius the Areopagite the ranks of the angels are nine in number. The throne which stands raised on steps is the image of the omnipotent Divine Spirit.

> The mysteries of this church, which tell of heaven and earth, are lofty: in them the most Holy Trinity and the saving plan of our Saviour are represented....

In early Christendom, therefore, two completely different types of cathedral confronted one another: the long-shaped basilica (in which the relationship between the here-below and the beyond is represented in a horizontal manner by means of a lengthy nave leading from forecourt to apse) and the cupola-type construction (in which the cupola surmounts a central space, thus representing the relationship of Heaven and earth in a vertical manner). The first type remained predominant in Latin Christendom. In Greek Orthodox Christendom, on the other hand, the cupola type became the principal, if not the only, prototype. This choice is only partly explained in terms of the respective liturgies of the two churches. It is more an expression of two attitudes of soul: the Latin disposition is more directed towards forward-looking action, whether in outward works or *ascesis*, whereas the Eastern Christian disposition is directed more towards vision or contemplation. The cupola of a Byzantine church, such as Hagia Sophia, evokes the image of Heaven soaring above the earth; it is the symbol of the

Facing page
Chartres cathedral from the north-east. It stands on slightly raised ground in the midst of the wheat-fields of the plain of Beauce. Its foundations cover a grotto with a spring, which probably was already a sanctuary in pre-Christian times. Since the early Middle Ages a church stood on this spot. It was several times destroyed, and always re-built in larger dimensions right up to the thirteenth century cathedral, which, for its part, only narrowly escaped destruction during the French Revolution. In the last few centuries, the city has lost its earlier importance, becoming a provincial city which to this day retains its eighteenth century character.

all-enlightening Divine Presence, and to this also corresponds the fact that the Eastern liturgy always presents itself as a participation in the divine praise of the angels, which finds it most direct expression in the ejaculation: 'Holy! Holy! Holy!'.

In a certain sense, all later developments in church architecture in East and West result from the effort to combine the two types – the 'elongated' basilica and the 'concentrated' cupola construction – with each other.

Longitudinal section of the Church of the Holy Wisdom (*Hagia Sophia*) in Constantinople (Istanbul) in its original Byzantine form.

The most brilliant example of a cupola construction which, without infringing the all-inclusive unity of the vaulted space, assumed the long shape of a basilica, is Hagia Sophia in Constantinople: the powerful cupola which surmounts it in the centre, is extended towards east and west by five additional half cupolas, without the various vaultings being separated from one another by anything more than narrow ridges, and this confers on the overall interior space a feeling of infinitude that escapes all measure. It has this effect all the more strongly because the two apses, covered by half cupolas, are themselves recessed with smaller niches, while a ring of windows, like a luminous string of pearls, transpierces the main cupola just above the level where it rests on its support. From these high windows light streams onto the partition walls so that the cupola, as a Byzantine poet said,

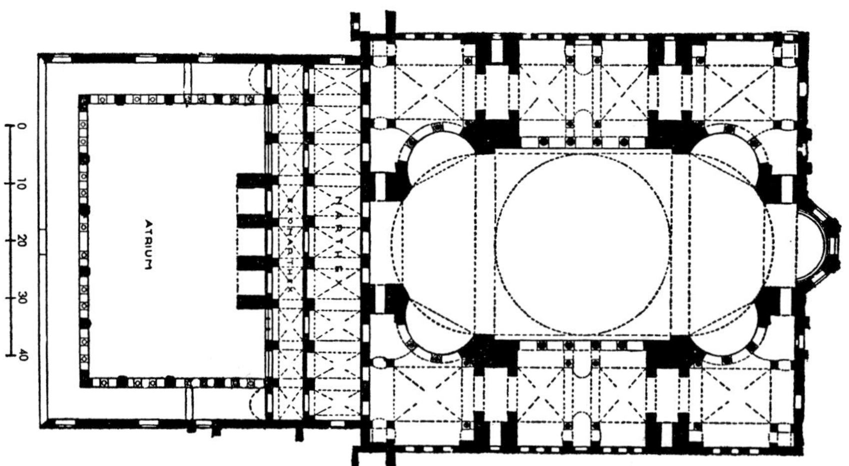

Groundplan of Hagia Sophia.

'seems not to rest on a solid foundation, but, attached to Heaven by a golden chain, crowns the underlying space'.[6] Another poet of the sixth century describes the almost dizzying width with the words:

> As soon as someone enters the sanctuary, he is filled with bliss, but also with disquiet and astonishment, as if he had entered Heaven itself, without anyone offering him resistance; surrounded on all sides by innumerable beautiful things, as if by stars, he is completely enchanted.[7]

The main nave, with its several recesses, is enclosed by a rectangle formed by the outside walls; the balance between the round and square plans can be seen in the aisles and the galleries, whose delicate partitions, transpierced by light, remove the measurable and perceptible limits of the main space. When a Byzantine poet says, of the fullness of light in the vast inner space of the church, that it seems that 'the space is not illumined by the sun from without, but rather the illumination originates within',[8] he is expressing an artistic ideal which Gothic architecture also sought to realize in its own way, by the introduction of transparent walls of stained glass. The Gothic architects must have heard much about the architectural miracle of Hagia Sophia, since Constantinople was a halting-place and advance post of the crusades; but it remained a distant model, which no one dared to imitate formally.

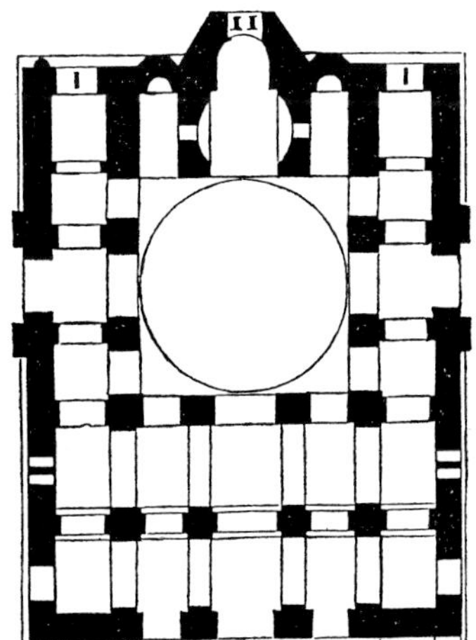

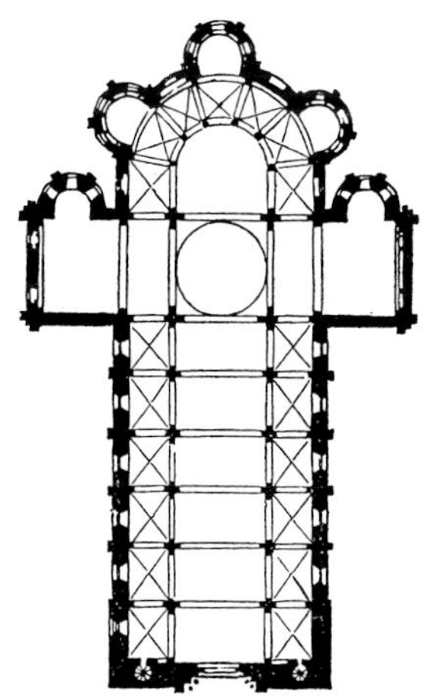

Groundplans of the Byzantine Church of St. Nicodemus in Athens and of the Romanesque Church of St. Stephen in Nevers.

While church architecture in the East preferred to take its starting point from the concentric cupola-space—which could be extended by the addition of side areas in the four directions of the cross—Latin architecture generally proceeded the other way round: it retained the elongated basilican plan, but introduced the cupola into this, in order to mark out the central area represented by the intersection of nave and transept.

> Jesus answered and said unto them, Destroy this temple, and in three days I will raise it up. Then said the Jews, Forty and six years was this temple in building, and wilt thou rear it up in three days? But he spake of the temple of his body. (*John*, II:19–21)

These words of Christ make the church building symbolically the body of the God-man. According to Church Fathers such as Augustine and Theodoret, Christ compares His body to the Temple of Jerusalem, not because He was its reflection, but because the temple was the reflection of His body; from the temporal point of view, the Temple of Solomon is indeed the 'model' of the earthly body of the Lord, but the latter is, in a much truer sense than the temple of stone, the dwelling-place of God. Thus in principle the body of Christ is the model for all constructed sanctuaries.

On the other hand, the building of the Church, which according to the words of Christ is founded on a rock, consists of the community of believers. 'Ye also, as lively stones, are built up a spiritual house.' (I *Peter*, II:5) The medieval writers transpose this to the church building: Honorius Augustodunensis writes:

> This house is founded on a rock, just as the Church rests on the firm foundation stone of Christ. Its four walls rise up, just as the Church, thanks to the four Gospels, grows upwards.... The stones are held together by mortar, just as the believers are united by the bond of love.... The pillars which support the building are the bishops... The beams which strengthen its walls are the worldly princes who endow the Church.... The tiles which keep out the rain are the warriors who protect the Church from her enemies.... The floor on which one walks is the people who maintain the Church with their work. The subterranean crypts are those people who practise a spiritual life.... The altar on which sacrifice is made, is Christ.[9]

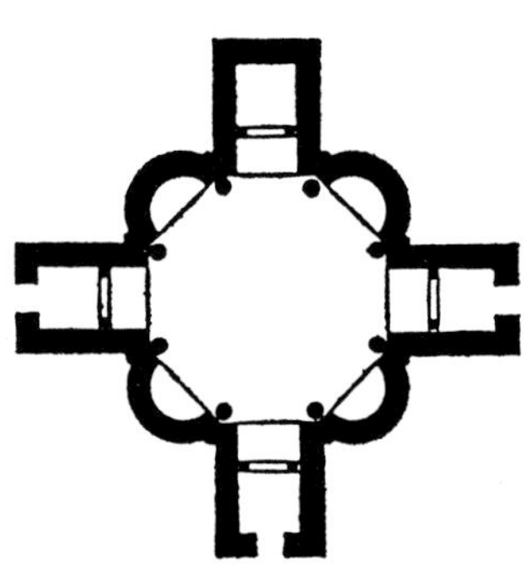

Groundplan of the cruciform Church of St. Gregory, at Nyssa, Asia Minor.

Thus the sacred building resembles the Christian community, which for its part represents the body of Christ. There is also a visible similarity between the church building and the human form of the Saviour. This becomes plain when the groundplan of the church, as in Romanesque minsters and Gothic cathedrals, takes the form of a Latin cross: 'The disposition of the built church,' writes Durand de Mende, 'corresponds to the human body; for the choir, or the place where the altar is situated, represents the head, the north and south transepts correspond to the arms and hands, and the nave, extended to the west, corresponds to the rest of the body....'[10] When the main altar, as is often the case, is situated at the intersection of the nave and the transept, it corresponds to the heart in the body of the Divine Man.

At an early stage, there were cruciform churches in Asia Minor which contained the tombs of martyrs. The Latin basilicas, with the apse directly connected to the transept, at first resembled a T more than a cross. Most similar to the cross of the Passion is the groundplan of the late-Romanesque abbey churches, where the transept extends widely and the choir is lengthened by the insertion of a straight section between the transept and the apse. This development in the groundplan was to meet a liturgical need. It provided room for a number of altars, at which several priests of the monastic community could celebrate their masses at the same time. However, the similarity of the form of the church to the body of the crucified Saviour is too significant not to have been consciously intended, even though at that period no one would have dreamt of painting or constructing this similarity naturalistically.

The body of Christ inscribed in the groundplan of the church is as if affixed to the cross formed by the axes of the heavens: His head lies towards the east, His feet towards the west, His arms and hands extend from north to south. This identification of the cross of the heavens with the cross of the Passion is also founded on ecclesiastical tradition: according to the Church Fathers Hieronymus and Basilius, the axial cross of the heavens is the preordained prototype of the martyr's wood on which the Saviour was nailed. Today it would be said that the

Facing page
Man as the 'little world' (*microcosmos*) in the centre of the spheres of the 'big world' (*macrocosmos*); taken from a miniature in a manuscript of the writings of St. Hildegard of Bingen (Codex 1942) in the State Library at Lucca. Man, in whom the powers and properties of the universe (*cosmos*) are united, is represented standing in front of the globe, while the 'big world', for its part, is enclosed by a human form—a sign that man and world correspond to one another as image and reflection. Above everything appears the face of an old man, the creative spirit, who rules over both macrocosm and microcosm.

Christological meaning had been subsequently transposed from the instrument of the Passion to the astronomical cross; but it is the Church Fathers who are right, not only from the spiritual, but also from the historical point of view. For the people of antiquity the cross of the axes of the heavens was the direct expression of cosmic law; if a transgressor against this law—or against its application in society—was executed on a cross, this was in order to re-establish, both symbolically and practically, the disturbed cosmic equilibrium.

The human figure as the basis for the groundplan of a church, after Francesco di Giorgio. Manuscript in the Biblioteca Laurenziana, Florence.

Essentially, the cosmic law is an equilibrium of opposites, which either exclude each other or reciprocally complement each other, and whose relationships, referred to a centre, are most easily represented in the form of a cross. The permanent characteristics or 'powers' of the sensible world—the four elements (fire, air, water, earth), with the corresponding four temperaments (choleric, sanguine, phlegmatic, and melancholic); and the four natural qualities (dry, hot, wet, and cold) with the four corresponding seasons (spring, summer, autumn, and winter)—can be represented by two crosses, one diagonal and one upright, as shown below. This manner of perceiving the cosmic attributes can also be applied to the animic (i.e. psychic) and spiritual realms. The cosmologists of antiquity and of the Middle Ages, who thought in terms of the great cosmic analogies, ordered things according to this basic groundplan of all discrimination.

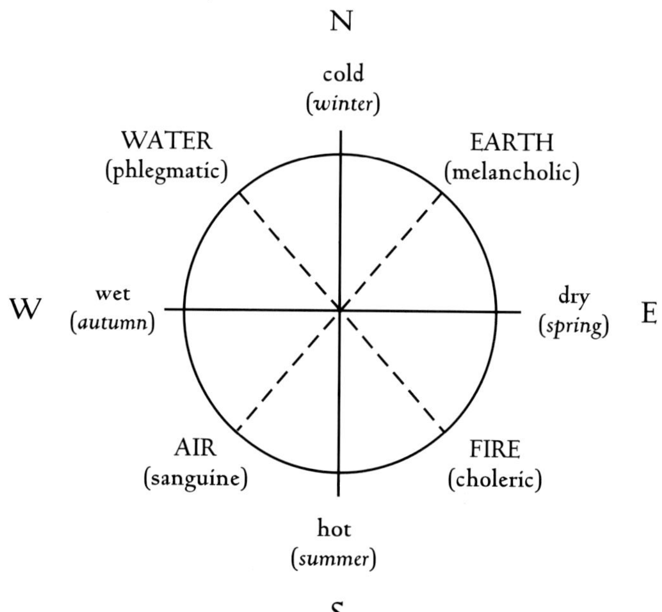

The Church Fathers teach that, for the divine nature of Christ, the Incarnation was already a sacrifice, a voluntary limitation of itself, and so a kind of crucifixion. In its self-lowering, the divine nature took upon itself the cross of a world that is compounded of opposites. The actual crucifixion of Christ thus appears as the inevitable outward result of the Incarnation; it represents fulfilment of the cosmic law, and at the same time inward victory over it.

The liturgy for the consecration of a church, the form of which can be traced back to the early Middle Ages, expressly compares the sacred edifice to the Heavenly Jerusalem. This contradicts none of the previously mentioned symbolisms, for the Heavenly Jerusalem represents that final condition of existence in which everything in the world that is theomorphic, and therefore essentially indestructible, is 'caught up' out of time and into the eternal Divine Spirit (1 *Thess.*,

IV:17). The Heavenly City is thus also compared to a unique, immutable, and shining jewel:

> And the angel carried me away in the spirit to a great and high mountain, and shewed me that great city, the holy Jerusalem, descending out of Heaven from God, having the glory of God: and her light was like unto a stone most precious, even like a jasper stone, clear as crystal. (*Apocalypse*, XXI:10–11)

The Divine City descends from Heaven, because, as prototype of the human condition, it was always present in the Divine Spirit; it is also the goal or endpoint of time.

Whereas the temporal world can be represented as an endless circular movement, the Divine City, in its immutable perfection, resembles a cube:

> And the city lieth foursquare, and the length is as large as the breadth . . . the length and the breadth and the height of it are equal. (*Apocalypse*, XXI:16)

The walls of the city correspond to the vault of Heaven traversed by the sun, for they have twelve doors, just as Heaven has twelve 'signs' or 'houses':

> And the city had a wall great and high, and had twelve gates, and at the gates twelve angels, and names written thereon, which are the names of the twelve tribes of the children of Israel. (*Apocalypse*, XXI:12)

Likewise it has twelve foundations, corresponding to the twelve Apostles. Because, however, the city is shaped like a cube, the circle of the sun's orbit, transposed to static and timeless mode, has been converted into a square:

> On the east three gates, on the north three gates, on the south three gates; and on the west three gates. (*Apocalypse*, XXI:13)

The figures given for the dimensions of the city also point to the transmutation of all time into a single present resting in itself: the angel measured the extent of the city as 'twelve thousand furlongs' and the height of its walls as 'one hundred and forty-four cubits'. (*Apocalypse*, XXI:16–17) Both of these are solar numbers, derived from the precession of the equinoxes, the greatest measure of all cosmic movements: the time it takes for the two equinoxes to change positions in the heaven of fixed stars is exactly 12,960 years; the figure 12,000, corresponding to the 'great year' of the Persians, relates this duration to the solar year of twelve months; 144 is a factor of 12,960. Thus the Heavenly City incorporates the whole of time by transmuting it, as in were, into space.

The Heavenly City is made of substances that have shed every trace of corruptibility, substances that are neither mutable nor opaque, but immutable and as if made of solidified light:

> And the building of the wall of it was of jasper: and the city was pure gold, like unto clear glass. And the foundations of the wall of the city were garnished with all manner of precious stones. The first foundation was jasper; the second, sapphire; the third, a chalcedony; the fourth, an emerald; the fifth, sardonyx; the sixth, sardius; the seventh, chrysolyte; the eighth, beryl; the ninth, a topaz; the tenth, a chrysoprasus; the eleventh, a jacinth; the twelfth, an amethyst.

> And the twelve gates were twelve pearls: every several gate was of one pearl: and the street of the city was pure gold, as it were transparent glass.
>
> And I saw no temple therein: for the Lord God Almighty and the Lamb are the temple of it.
>
> And the city had no need of the sun, neither of the moon, to shine in it: for the glory of God did lighten it, and the Lamb is the light thereof. (*Apocalypse*, XXI:18–23)

The Heavenly Jerusalem is the counterpart of the earthly paradise; the latter is at the beginning, the former at the end of time. The image of the earthly paradise is spring, flowering trees, running streams, singing birds, and playing animals, whereas the Heavenly Jerusalem, as the image of fulfilment, is completely static; everything in it is made from minerals, gold and precious stones. Ecclesiastical architecture has taken its symbolism as much from the one as from the other. Not only do the 'paradises' of the Romanesque and Carolingian basilicas, and the transepts of the Romanesque minsters, remind one of the Garden of Eden, but the vegetable motifs decorating the capitals also point to the paradisal spring. But even more important for architecture, and more deeply related to its essence, was the model of the crystalline Heavenly City.

The symbol of a perfect city or a perfect building as epitome of the timeless perfection of all things derives from such a deep and universal vision, and corresponds so completely to the spiritual essence of all architecture, that it must inevitably also be found outside the Christian tradition; in fact, it is present in every theocratic culture. It appears most clearly, and in a form most closely related to the Christian one, in Hinduism. The groundplan of the Indian temple is founded on a geometrical scheme which transposes the cosmic orbits, both solar and lunar, into a regular and chequered square, whose peripheral areas (which correspond to the signs of the zodiac) are, like the 'gates' of the Heavenly Jerusalem, ruled by angels or *devas*, while its centre, which is looked on as the source of all light, represents the 'place or locus of God' (*Brahmâsthana*).[11]

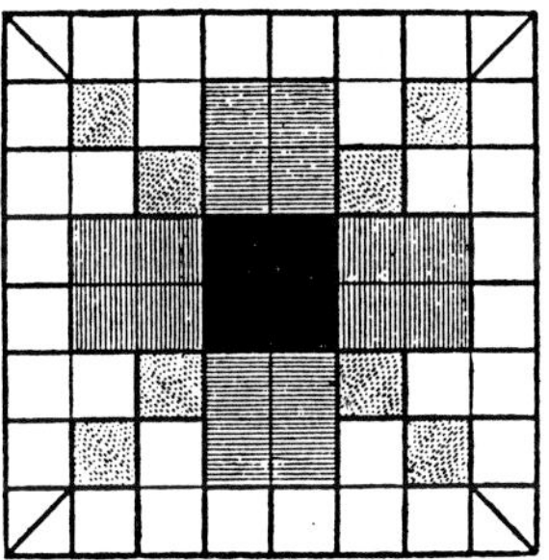

A mandala forming the basis for Hindu temple architecture, composed of 9 × 9 fields.

The same symbolism appears again in some Buddhist meditation pictures, on which, inside the circle that represents the endless cycle of becoming and unbecoming, there is a square resembling a palace or a city with its gates. In the centre of this, an image of the Enlightened One sits on a throne. This brings us back to a Christian view, expounded by St. Augustine and other Church Fathers, according to which passion and sin wander around in a circular motion, while the righteous soul, formed by the cardinal virtues, is 'square', like a regularly chiselled foundation stone.

In view of this, it might be asked why churches never assumed the form of cubes. There are indeed Byzantine churches whose rectangular form does approximate to that of a cube, as well as Ethiopian churches hewn from rock which are almost cubic, but these are exceptions. The reason is that a cubic inner space did not cater for either the Greek or the Latin liturgy; and, in any case, the church building did not have to imitate the prototype of the Heavenly City absolutely literally; it was itself on earth and in time. Strictly speaking, only the Holy of Holies could correspond to the Heavenly Jerusalem, just as did the Holy of Holies of the Temple of Solomon, which in fact was cubic in shape. Medieval Christians always accepted symbols as symbols, without sticking slavishly to the letter, and this accounts for the fact, amongst others, that a large number of Romanesque

Facing page
Type of painted crucifix commonly found on the triumphal arches of Italian churches of the twelfth and thirteenth centuries, by the Master of St Francis. Here the crucifix is itself both a vehicle for paintings and a geometrical figure reminiscent of the groundplan of a church. The inscription in the top terminal would originally have read, in Latin, 'Behold, this is Jesus Christ, King of the Jews, Saviour of the World and our Salvation, who for us hung on the Tree of Life'.

chandeliers, through their figured jewelry as well as through the inscriptions they bore, were looked on as images of the Heavenly Jerusalem. That in the church, which itself was the image of the Heavenly Jerusalem, a second symbol with the same significance was to be found, disturbed no one.

Let us now return to the rite of orientation, which sums up all the basic forms, and thus all the essential meanings, of the sacred building: according to ancient sources, including Indian and Chinese manuals, the writings of Vitruvius, and also some late Gothic documents,[12] the orientation of the groundplan of a building could best be achieved in the following manner: on the levelled building site, a stave of wood is inserted vertically and, by means of a piece of string, one draws a circle resembling a sundial. This has to be wide enough for the shadow of the end of the stave to touch the circle early in the morning and again at a corresponding hour in the evening. The two points where the shadow touches the circle are marked with wooden pegs and, once again with the help of a piece of string, one marks out from them two equally large intersecting circles. The 'fish' formed by their intersection gives the exact position of the midday line; it runs through the middle of the main circle in which the stave stands. If one now applies the string to the intersections of the midday line with the main circle, one can mark the west-east line and thus obtain the axial cross, from which the various corners of the groundplan can be determined.

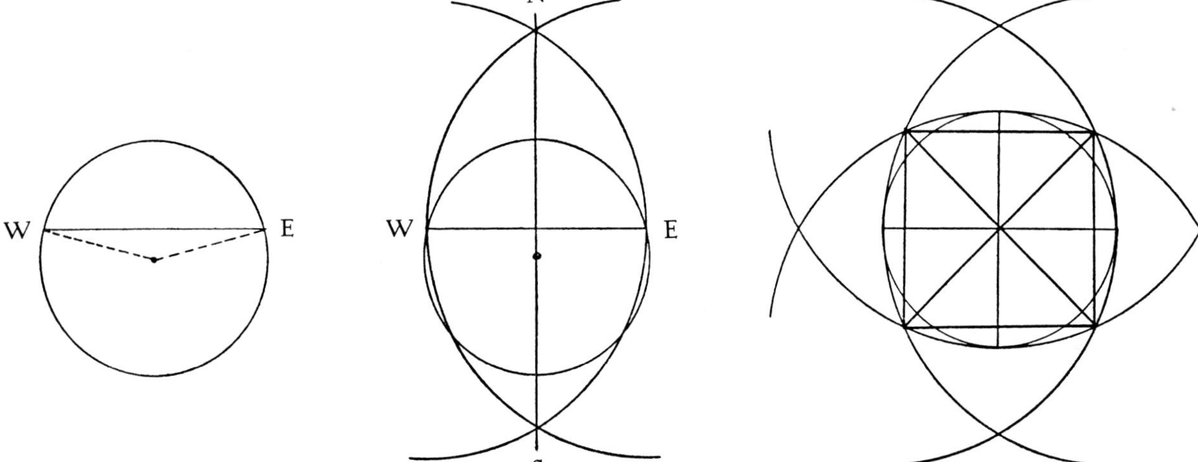

Essentially the process of orientation consists in deriving the rectangle of the sacred building from the circle traced by the course of the sun by means of the cross of the axes of Heaven. If one conceives the circle as the visible trace of time, the obtaining of a rectangle from it represents the transmutation of time into a spiritual 'space', and this corresponds to the image of the Heavenly Jerusalem, which at the end of time descends from Heaven like a perfected cube.

The Preliminary Stages

IF ONE LOOKS on the Gothic cathedral as the highpoint and final outcome of Medieval architecture—which would be a one-sided but not entirely unjustified point of view—the development that led to this outcome would seem to start with the first attempts to surmount the basilican churches with vaults. This occurred in the early Romanesque period. Until then, the early Christian elongated form had scarcely changed. Carolingian art had consciously imitated the imperial Roman model, altering it only outwardly, by providing the nave with towers, and building up its western façade rather like a fortress. In the Germanic north, where the last waves of the tribal migrations still surged, and where no distinction was made between city and fortress, the City of God must also have had this allure. The first Gothic cathedrals were to raise this Carolingian form of church exteriors to an expression of angelic might.

The west front of the Romanesque abbey of Marialaach in the Rhineland, in which a Carolingian influence can be seen. In front of the west choir is a courtyard surrounded by pillars, the so-called 'paradise'.

The vaulting of a church answered to a need, for all too often it happened that a church roofed over with beams fell victim to fire. The early Romanesque basilicas were usually adorned with wall-hangings; how easily the flame of a flickering candle could reach a wall-hanging and, surging upwards, set fire to the beams! Since, however, in medieval art, there is no form that has only a practical purpose and does not at the same time serve as a spiritual expression, one can safely assume that the covering vault always possessed the meaning of the vault of Heaven. This is proved by the pictures with which it was decorated.

The development of the various forms of vaulting conferred on Romanesque architecture its special character as well as its variety which, from the Gothic point of view, must have seemed rather like blind trial and error. In reality, each stage and each variation in building style gave rise to masterpieces, which, in their kind, were never surpassed. In order to bring a particular combination of forms to perfection, other no less precious forms have to be sacrificed. The Gothic style sacrificed as much as it gained. Nevertheless, leaving aside various side branches, one can discern a straight line of development from early Romanesque to Gothic.

The easiest way to cover an elongated building with stone was by means of barrel vaulting. This conferred on the nave, which ended at the east with a niche-like apse, the aspect of a cave, all the more so since the walls were provided with very few windows: the heavy pressure of the unarticulated barrel on the side walls was too great to allow them to be penetrated by windows. Since, however, the cave is one of the most ancient forms of sanctuary, and is endowed with this meaning so universally, the similarity of which we speak and which impresses itself so strongly on all who visit early Romanesque churches, could not possibly have been mere accident. According to a tradition well-known in the Christian East as well as in the Western Middle Ages, Christ was born in a cave, and this cave was understood both as a metaphor for this world of darkness and as an image of the heart. This indeed is the meaning of every sacred cave: it is the universe turned inward, the secret world of the heart or of the soul, in which earth, Heaven, and all things are prefigured, and which is illumined by the Divine Sun of the Spirit. The sacred cave is one of those timeless symbols which, without visible historical tradition, can manifest anywhere and at any time. Early Romanesque churches resembling caves are to be found in the region of the Pyrenees.

The barrel vault of the early Romanesque church of Montbui in Catalonia.

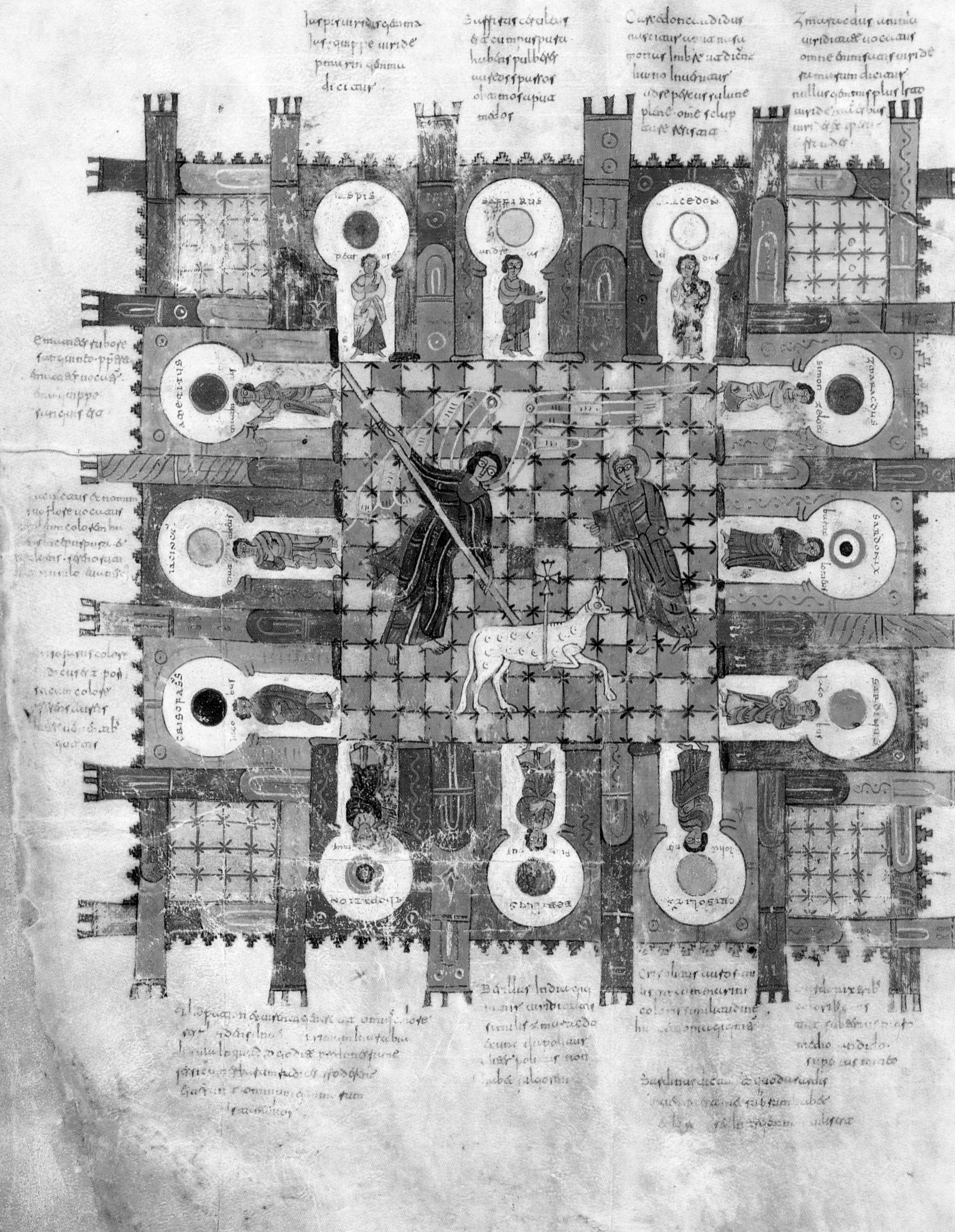

The pressure of barrel vaulting on the side walls can be lessened by ribs spanning the nave, which were carried on pilasters. Thus the walls between the pilasters bore much less weight and could be penetrated by windows. Barrel vaulting could also be improved by raising its vertex to form a pointed arch. This architectural form was continued up to the arrival of Gothic and, in Cistercian churches, became the hallmark of an ascetically simple and at the same time noble style.

Instead of covering the nave with a barrel vault, one could also cover it with several cupolas, which rested on transverse arches and supported themselves on pilasters by means of funnel-shaped squinches. In this way the interior space is divided into several 'heavens', which are compensated for by the simplicity of the groundplan. This style, common in south-western France, the ancient Aquitaine, resembles the Byzantine, and thus represents a side-branch from the main stream of Romanesque art. Individual cupolas are also to be found in typically Romanesque basilicas, like gigantic ciboriums above the altar, covered by the transept tower.

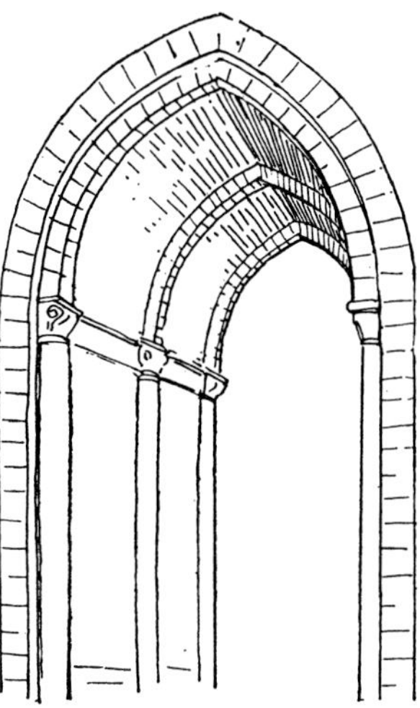

Barrel vault with pointed arch and wall supports.

Barrel vault on wall supports in the Romanesque church at Corbera in Catalonia.

When barrel vaulting spanned a nave that had aisles on each side, its vertical pressure bore down upon the arcades, and its lateral thrust had to be directed onto the outer walls. With this end in view, the aisles were often covered with half-vaults which in cross-section resemble quarter-arches and serve the same function as do later the flying buttresses visible on the outside of Gothic cathedrals. One can see how flying buttresses developed: the half-vaults over the aisles were stripped of their roofs and broken up into individual ribs, with a view to disencumbering the clerestory of the main nave.

In those cases where both the nave and the transept of a church were covered with simple round barrel vaults, there arose from their mutual intersection a cross vault with ridges which directed the weight of the roof not onto the side walls, but

Facing page
The Heavenly Jerusalem, a miniature in a tenth century Spanish manuscript. The interior of the city is as if seen from above, and is surrounded by outward-facing walls. In the centre are the Lamb of God, St. John with the Gospel, and the Angel with his staff measuring the city. Beneath the twelve gates are the Apostles, and above the gates are pearls, with which Holy Scripture compares the gates. The whole plan of the city is developed from a chessboard-like area composed of 12 × 12 fields, which yields the solar figure of 144, the number measured by the angel.

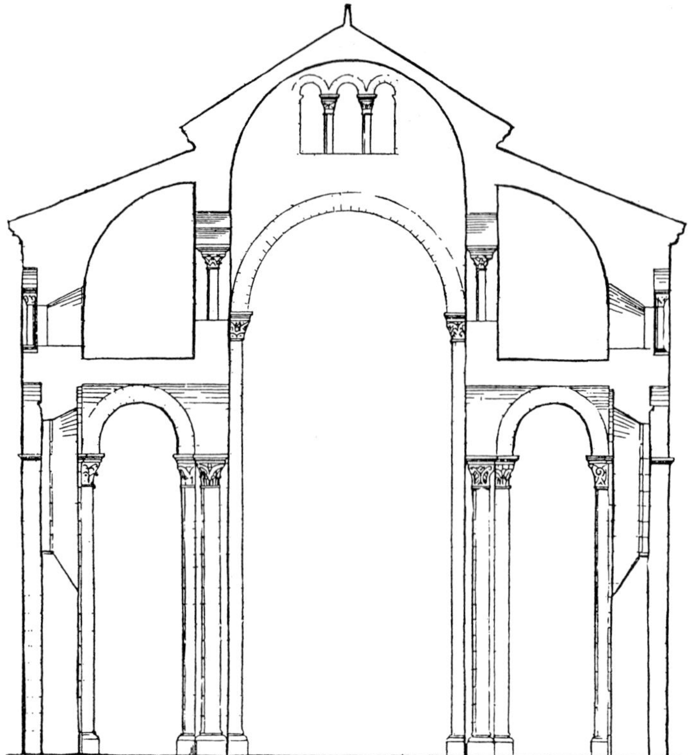

Cross-section of the nave of the Romanesque church of Notre-Dame-du-Port at Clermont-Ferrand.

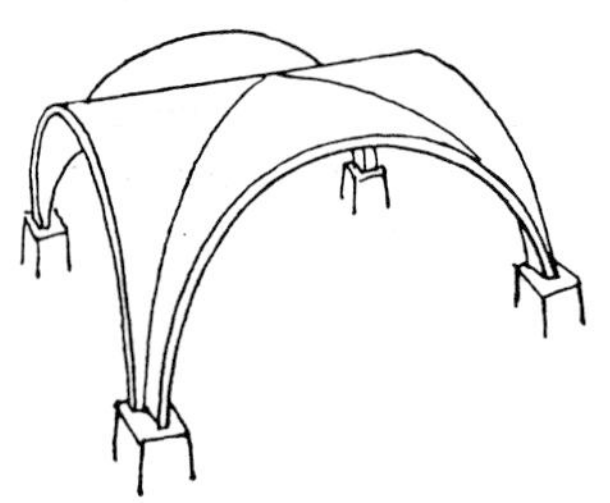

Scheme of a cross vault of quadratic type.

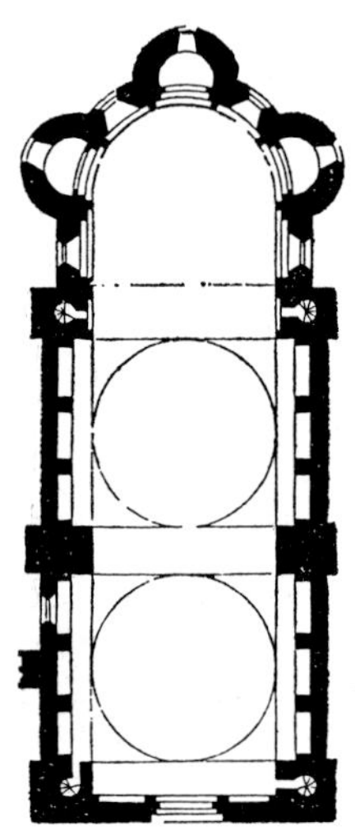

Groundplan of Cahors cathedral, surmounted by cupolas.

onto the piers at four corners of the said intersection. The plan of such a cross vault is square, while each of the four sides of the square appears in elevation as a round arch. When a nave is covered with a series of cross vaults, which meet on ribs and whose thrust is directed towards the walls onto so-called nave arcades, there remains under these arcades a wall which is only slightly loaded and which consequently is available for windows. The principal weight of the vault lies on the corners, where the ridges run together with the ribs and the arcades, and are supported more or less indirectly by the pillars of the arcades. If the aisles are also covered with cross vaults, there results, thanks to the square plan of the vault, a rhythmical alternation of supports, in that each bay of the nave has the breadth of two bays in an aisle. The plan of one of the smaller cross vaults is thus a quarter the area of a large one. This arrangement, based on square vaults, is called the 'grid system', and the manner of construction of Gothic arches, which is not based on these square formations, is regarded as an artistic liberation. However, the unitary Romanesque pattern has the advantage that the viewer can, with his inward eye, complete even those parts of the inner space which, at a given moment, elude his view.

Therein indeed lies the superiority of Romanesque art: thanks to its geometrically simple and spatially enclosed forms, a Romanesque minster always created an effect of unity and greatness, even when it is reduced to the size of a model. A Gothic church, on the other hand, is great in relation to man, above whom it soars like a mountain or a high forest.

If one looks at the cross vault as such, along with the four pillars on which it rests, it can be seen to resemble a baldachin. On all four sides, further baldachins can be added, so that the space that is vaulted can be extended to the degree desired. This was a means of construction that Gothic architecture was to exploit to the full. Its immediate effect in Romanesque architecture was that the aisles around the intersection of nave and transept were extended beyond and around the choir. The wall of the choir was thus lightened by arcades, and resulted, here at the head of the church, in a kind of concentric-cum-radial arrangement.

This arrangement strongly resembled the plan of the Church of the Holy Sepulchre and the Dome of the Rock in Jerusalem. As in these cases, the ambulatory served the needs of the stream of pilgrims, who circumambulated a relic. In the early Middle Ages it was the custom to conserve relics in church crypts and to venerate them there. In places where pilgrims constantly flocked, subterranean ambulatories were constructed, from which the tombs or relics could be viewed through openings. From the eleventh to the twelfth century, however, when the whole life of the church began to be directed more towards the outward – at the same time as the first figurative representations of the Divinity appeared on doors and façades – the cult of relics rose from below the earth, and with it the choir ambulatory, to meet the light of day.

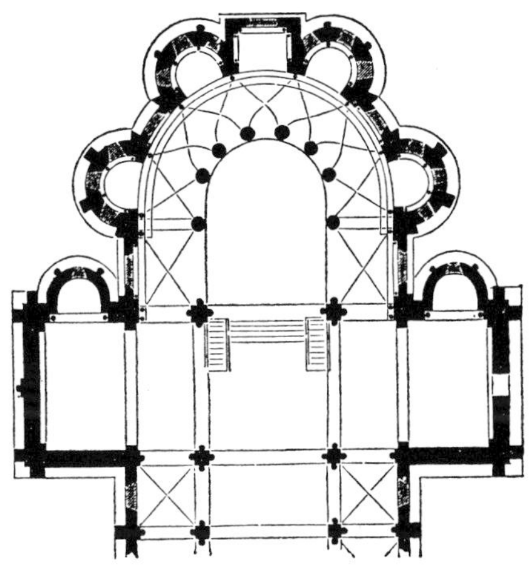

Groundplan of the choir of the Romanesque church at Issoire in the Auvergne and of the rotunda of the Church of the Holy Sepulchre in Jerusalem; after Viollet-le-Duc.

The custom of circumambulating a holy place is itself immemorial and goes back to pre-Christian times, as does the corresponding architectural form, the ambulatory, which is already to be found in early Hindu temples. It is characteristic of medieval Christian culture that it re-animates customs and forms that go back to prehistoric times, and assimilates them into its own perspective.

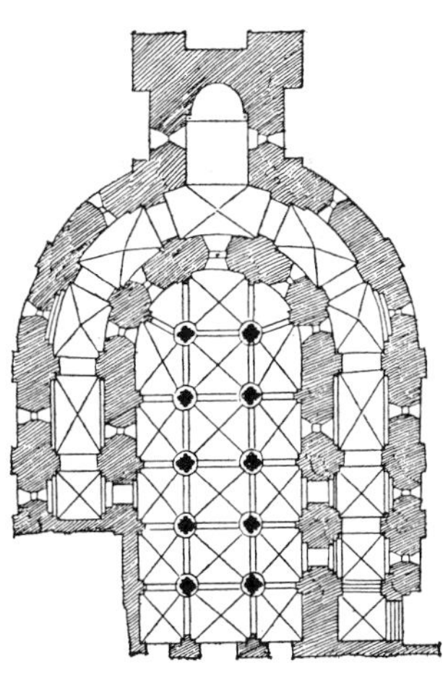

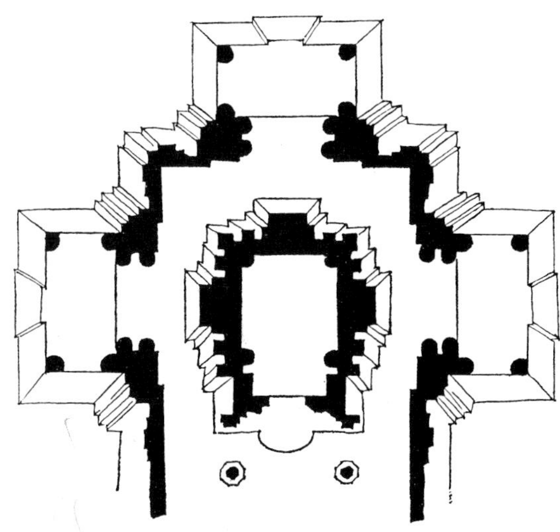

Groundplans of the crypt of the early Romanesque cathedral of Auxerre and of the 'ambulatory' (*pradakshina*) around the holy of holies in a Hindu temple.

Here a word must be said about the veneration of relics, which played such an important role in the Middle Ages. It is based on the scriptural teaching that, at the Last Judgement, not only souls, but also bodies, will be resurrected, so that, for example, the bones of a saint or martyr may represent as it were a piece of earth which, within the measure of the possible, participates in the bliss of Paradise. The theologically instructed man of the Middle Ages certainly knew that it was not the earthly and material body that would be resurrected, since the 'glorious body' of the blessed in Paradise is not spatially limited; only the essence of the body is immortal, namely its archetypal 'form', which participates in the wholeness of Being. Yet there does exist a certain relationship between the mortal remains of a saint and that which he is in eternity. Already on earth, his body is no longer merely opaque and heavy matter: it has already been touched by that very breath which, at the end of time, will transmute all matter into its eternal principle.

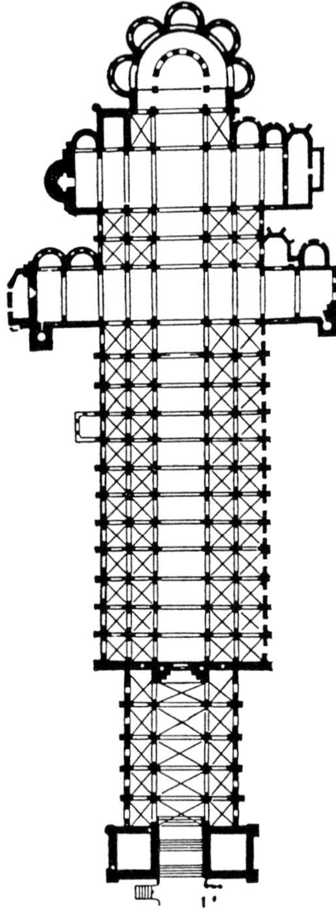

Groundplan of the late Romanesque abbey of Cluny; after Viollet-le-Duc.

℄

The late Romanesque basilica, especially as constructed by the Cluniac monks, developed, in all six directions of space, into such a richly articulated structure that the need for a clarifying synthesis became apparent: the choir with its ambulatory, the light-shaft of the tower at the crossing of nave and transept, and the transepts with their lateral aisles and choir-like side chapels, all had more and more receded from the general view. Even vertically, the central nave was divided into different zones: above the arcades, usually, were the raised galleries; above these, at the level of the roof over the aisles, was the triforium; and above this was the clerestory with windows. Gothic was to restore spatial unity, not by renouncing the complex articulation – development never returns to the starting-point – but, in a completely new and hitherto unknown way, by surrounding the over-extended spatial layout with a light, transparent shell. The shady areas disappeared, the partition walls became light, and the roof soared above all else.

All this became possible only because of new forms of vaulting, which rested exclusively on the pillars and no longer required supporting walls. For this purpose, the Romanesque cross vault was too heavy and stiff; its weakness was that the groins, whose function was to direct the weight onto the four pillars, were not in the form of complete semicircles, but of compressed arches. Anything else would have been impossible: if the lateral arches, corresponding to cross-sections of the mutually intersecting barrels, had been in the form of perfectly round arches, the diagonal groins would have had to be flatter. Furthermore, in vaults that were not entirely square, the groins, being the intersection lines of the unequal half-cylinders, were not, on plan, straight lines, but had to be curved.

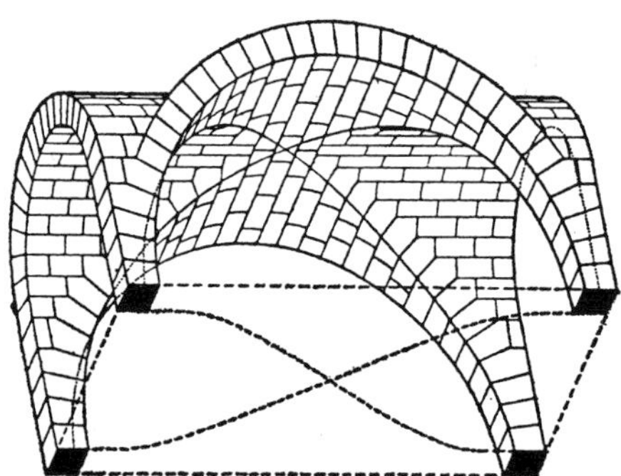

Scheme of a longitudinal cross-vault; after John Fitchen.

Two elements made the lightly spanned baldachins of Gothic churches possible: the pointed arch and rib vaulting. Gothic did not invent these, but was the first to put them to use for this purpose. The pointed arch makes it possible for the pilasters and nave arcades to rise as steeply as may be desired and to have different spans; if indeed they are steep enough, the ribs, having the same vertical height, can take the form of pure semicircles. In plan, they appear as straight lines, for they do not follow, as does the groin of the cross vault, the intersection lines of two mutually intersecting barrels, but form ideal curves; they are a purely linear arrangement, one which determines the shape of the more or less strongly curved arches resting upon them. These leap and cavort wildly between the varyingly wide, sometimes round, sometimes pointed, arches of the building skeleton.

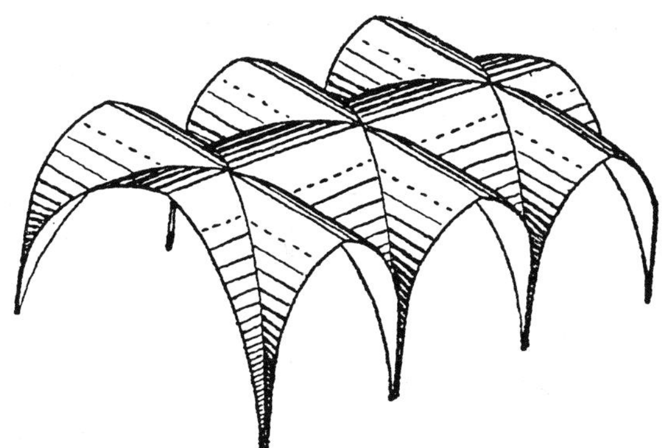

Gothic vaulting; after John Fitchen

In this, the Gothic style differs from the Romanesque: in the latter, a line is always derived from the meeting of two surfaces. Spatial form is there first, the line is derived from it, and consequently the inner space is always seen, as a receptacle, limited in extent by surfaces. Gothic architecture, on the other hand, takes the line as its starting-point, and extends it through space. Here space is no longer a receptacle, but an area of infinitely numerous relationships and tensions, as can be seen in the geometry of the building's articulations. The Gothic experience of space is speculative; point and line are not corporeal, but spiritual, elements; through their play, outward space is transmuted into intellectual space.

On the basis of this same perspective Gothic was also able to break through the solid body of the building to transform the walls into lattice-work and to let the supports of the vaulting spring up in the form of freestanding flying buttresses on the outside of the building.

The spiritual unity of the inner space, covered by a canopy of stone, is ensured by the fact that the outside walls, although transparent, do not have holes in them: the luminous curtain of stained glass protects the interior space from the profane outside world.

The church must not appear as if illuminated from without, but as if its walls, like the Heavenly Jerusalem, were fashioned out of self-luminous precious stones.

The Romanesque church building is earth in its lower reaches, Heaven in its height. Around the space in a Gothic church, Heaven itself descends like a mantle of crystalline light.

Left. Inner articulation of the nave of Rheims cathedral, from the sketchbook of the Picardian architect Villard de Honnecourt (thirteenth century).

Above. The supporting pillars and flying buttresses of Rheims cathedral, from the sketchbook of Villard de Honnecourt. This is a characteristic example of the Gothic tendency to transfer attention away from the solid building and towards its sinews and supports. The buttresses not only bear the lateral thrust of the vaulting, they also counteract pressure from the wind. In this example they suggest the rigging of a tent.

Church, Kingdom, and Art

IF CAROLINGIAN art reached its peak in the imperial cathedrals, and the mature Romanesque style in the abbey churches, the epitome of Gothic architecture, in its 'classical' phase, lies in the 'royal episcopal' cathedrals: the first Gothic cathedrals were built by bishops who, as spiritual and also temporal lords, were the principal supports of the Kingdom of France, freshly awakened to a new spiritual awareness.

The French Royal House had for long regarded itself as the true heir to Charlemagne and therefore as protector of the Church and champion of the faith. At the very time when the German emperor, through his prolonged altercation with the Pope, increasingly lost his status as leader of all western Christian peoples, the French King placed himself at the forefront of the crusades, championed the liberation of Spain from Moorish domination, encouraged the reformation of the Church, as had been demanded by St. Bernard of Clairvaux, and also generously granted new rights to the cities. Thus the golden ball of the fame of the French Royal House rolled forwards, and, without formally denying any of the emperor's prerogatives, it nevertheless strove to achieve sufficient power and prestige to ensure its complete independence from him. When, in order to justify his own independence from the Pope, the Emperor referred to Caesar (whose authority Christ had recognized with the words: 'Render unto Caesar the things that are Caesar's'), the spiritual defenders of the French King referred to the example of Old Testament kings, such as David and Solomon, who became leaders and judges of the Chosen People because the High Priest of God had anointed them. With this precedent in view, the French King was also consecrated by the highest dignitary in the Gallic Church with the holy oil conserved in Rheims. Thus to the Roman idea of empire, France opposed the biblical idea of a holy kingdom – there Caesar, here David! The 'royal doors' and the 'royal galleries' on the façades of the Gothic cathedrals are the biblical representation of this idea: the royal ancestors of Christ, who stand guard in front of the sanctuary, are at the same time the spiritual ancestors of the King of France.

The kingdom was holy; but not necessarily the king; medieval men could distinguish between the office and the holder. Because, however, the idea of a holy kingdom was more than just an abstract thought, it was inevitable that it would eventually find its perfect human expression; a phenomenon such as St. Louis,[13] despite all the imponderables with which such a man 'born of the spirit' is surrounded, is unthinkable without the prepared framework. Significantly, his appearance coincides with the perfection of Gothic architecture, as manifested, for example, by the Sainte-Chapelle in Paris. What follows later is decadence, of the kingdom as well as of art; but even the extent of this decadence, which continued right up to the French Revolution and the onset of nationalism, proves *a contrario* the greatness of the idea which the decadence did but erode and betray.

The King received his mandate from the Church. After the Bishop, in the name of God, had poured the holy oil on his head, 'he removed from him the sword of worldly knighthood and girded him with the sword for punishing evil-doers, crowned him with the royal diadem, and offered him the sceptre and the hand of justice, so that he would defend the Church and the poor ....'[14]

Scenes from a stained-glass window in Chartres cathedral depicting the life of Charlemagne; after J. B. A. Lassus, *Monographie de la Cathédrale de Chartres*, Paris, 1867.

The Church was wise enough not to regard this hierarchical relationship in a one-sided way: as soon as the most senior of the bishops had anointed and crowned the king, he knelt down before the king and pledged his loyalty as vassal. For, in so far as they themselves possessed worldly power, the bishops were no more than liege-lords of the king. Bishop Ivo of Chartres explained these relationships very precisely: spiritual shepherds must always be freely chosen by the Church, but, in order to be invested with a greater or smaller fief, they must take an oath of allegiance to the king.

Thus it transpired that the King and the princes of the Church were natural allies: the bishops found in the King a protector against the encroachments of autocratic nobles, and the king, in his efforts to unite under his crown the only loosely linked vassal territories, found his surest support in the bishops, who had no hereditary privileges to protect. Half of the princely college, which the King had to consult over important decisions, consisted of the bishops of Rheims, Laon, Langres, Châlons, Beauvais and Noyon – names which today remind us less of political power than of renowned Gothic cathedrals.

℄

The opposition between the two orders represented by the German Empire and the French Kingdom became more acute when, in 1107, Pope Pascal II, severely oppressed by the Emperor Henry V, sought refuge in France. The Emperor demanded of him that he should recognize his prerogative in the matter of selecting princes of the Church. A report on the conversation that took place in Châlons between the Pope and the Emperor's ambassador is provided by Suger,[15] who later, as Abbot of Saint-Denis, was to become the spiritual church-builder of the kingdom, but who, at that time, was the young cleric appointed by Louis VI to escort the Pope while he was in France. In the name of the Emperor, the Bishop of Trier had spoken as follows:

Further scenes (of the life of Charlemagne) from the same window.

> This is the message with which our Lord the Emperor has entrusted us: in the time of our predecessors, and in the time of apostolic men like Gregory the Great, it was generally accepted that, having regard for the rights of the Emperor, the selection of a spiritual prince took place in the following way: before any step regarding the election is taken publicly, the name of the candidate should be submitted to the Emperor; if the person is acceptable to him, his agreement must be obtained before the election, whereupon, in a canonical gathering, at the wish of the people, and with the agreement of the hierarchy and of the temporal lord of the region, the person elected will be announced. As soon as the one elected has been consecrated, freely and without simony, he must be brought before the Emperor in order to obtain from him the regalia, the investiture with the ring and the shepherd's crook, and swear the oath of allegiance. There is nothing unusual in this, for how else can one take possession of a city, a fortress, an estate, or anything else that is dependent on imperial sovereignty? If the Pope accepts this procedure, Empire and Church will remain closely linked, in prosperity and peace, to the glory of God.

After some consideration, the Pope replied to this through his spokesman the Bishop of Piacenza:

Since the Church has been redeemed by the precious blood of Jesus Christ, it can at no price fall back into slavery. If it were not possible for her to select a dignitary without first having to ask the Emperor, she would remain subject to him like a slave, and Christ would have died in vain. That the investiture with ring and crook should be undertaken by the Emperor, when these things belong to the altar, is an encroachment on the rights of God Himself. That the hands of a priest, consecrated to the body and blood of the Lord, should have to reach out to the hands of a layman, bloody by the use of the sword, stands in contradiction to the sacrament of holy orders....'

It was not a question of mere formality: the whole spiritual organization of the West was at stake. Louis VI and the French hierarchy took the side of the Pope. In 1118 Henry V was excommunicated by a synod called by the then Archbishop of Vienna (later Pope Calixtus II). As a result, six years later, in the summer of 1124, the Emperor tried to obtain his revenge by a surprise attack on France. Suger, now Abbot of Saint-Denis, reports:

Our Lord, King Louis, who had heard of the attack through good friends, carefully and courageously set about raising an army. He acted without waiting for the invading army to arrive, summoning his nobles and explaining his plans to them.

Various reports, and his own repeated experience, had taught him that St. Dionysius was the special protector and, after God, the incomparable defender of the kingdom. He therefore rushed to him [that is to say, to his tomb in the Abbey of Saint-Denis which was named after him] and implored him with all his heart, with prayers and with good deeds, that he should defend his kingdom, save the person of the King himself, and, as on previous occasions, offer resistance to the enemy. Finally, he also made use of the privilege, granted to the French in the case of a threat from a foreign foe, to place the relics of the saint and his companions on the altar (with a view to protecting it), and he had this done in his presence with great solemnity and humility. Furthermore, he received from the altar [from the hands of the Abbot himself] the banner of the county of Vexin [to which the Abbey belonged], and in the name of which he himself was the vassal of the Church. He took this banner, in accordance with his oath, as if he were receiving it from the hands of St. Dionysius himself. And when, with a small company, he hastened to meet the foe, he invited the whole of France to follow him.[16]

Thus for the first time the King, like a vassal, carried the famous oriflamme in the face of the enemy, but, in the eyes of his retinue, it was as if he were no less than the delegate of the holy protector of France. Suger writes:

From all sides, knights rushed to join the King; armies were sent, composed of men who were inspired by memories of ancient valour and past victories. We all gathered in Rheims, we were a mighty force....

But in fact there was no encounter with the army of the emperor, who, on hearing news of the rapid and general mobilization of the French forces, beat a retreat. The victory was regarded as no less great because of that. In the words of

Suger: 'It was considered just as great or even greater than if one had won it in battle man to man.'

But the honour was accorded to St. Dionysius and his tomb.

An odd coincidence of names led to the conflation of the first Bishop of Paris (who with his companions Rusticus and Eleutherius had suffered a martyr's death) with St. Dionysius the Areopagite, the great exponent of Christian symbolism. That these two should be the same person is, however, historically improbable, for, according to Gregory of Tours, the holy bishop who lies buried near Paris was killed about the year 250, whereas St. Dionysius, according to medieval belief, was the direct disciple of the Apostle Paul, and, according to modern opinion, a theologian of the fifth century. Be that as it may, thanks to the great veneration that the 'Apostle of the Franks' enjoyed, and because of the special relationship between the French Royal House and his tomb (Pippin, the first Carolingian, had been anointed at Saint-Denis and, from the time of the Merovingians, most of the French kings were laid to rest there), St. Dionysius' writings on 'the celestial and ecclesiastical hierarchies' and on 'the divine names' were accorded the authority of apostolic teachings. For medieval France this was of great significance – especially at the time that the Gothic style arose and, as an artistic – but not only as an artistic–movement, began to spread far beyond France. For the writings of St. Dionysius contain all that is necessary to provide art with an intellectual basis, not only in terms of object, but also in terms of forms, whose beauty reflects truth in a way that cannot be expressed in words. Dionysius was not the only one to teach these things, but no one else had expounded such a comprehensive doctrine of symbolism. It was not by chance that the Byzantine defenders of icons such as John of Damascus and Theodore of Studion referred back to him. The Gothic style, which in a sense was the answer to the Cistercian reform's opposition to splendour in the Church, likewise found its justification in the Dionysian doctrine of symbolism.

☾

The doctrine of Dionysius the Areopagite depends on an intellectual vision which sees all degrees of reality, from the highest choirs of angels down to the corporeal world, as so many more or less broken reflections of the unique Divine Light. Dionysius writes:

> All things which have a positive existence, whether as substance or as modalities, indeed all things which are possible, have in God their principle and origin, their prototype and law, their goal and their final purpose. As the one and supreme Principle, He does not exteriorize Himself and yet He communicates Himself.... As perfect Archetype, He shines imperfectly in creatures, imperfectly because of their inevitable incapacity, not because His goodness has any limits.[17]

This doctrine has been called Neoplatonic, because Plato had spoken of the eternal prototypes – the ideas – of mortal things, and because the perspective of the hierarchical radiation of the Divine Light is elaborated in broad outline by his spiritual successor Plotinus. In all accuracy, however, it must be said that this doctrine arises wherever the contemplative intellect, by recognizing the divine essence of beauty, is able, in a sense, to bridge the duality of Creator and creature, without thereby forgetting the immeasurable gulf that separates the former from the latter:

> God dwells in hearts, minds and bodies; in Heaven and on earth; He is eternally immutable in the world, around the world, above the world, above the heavens, above all existence; He is sun, star, fire and water, wind, thaw and cloud, cornerstone and rock; He is everything that is, and yet is no created thing.[18]

Such a profound and comprehensive vision of reality—one that is both discriminative and unitive—cannot be grasped by the purely ratiocinative activity of the mind; it is in keeping however with sacred art. In contemplation as in art, it is a question of discerning the eternal essences of forms, and not confusing them with the outward limits of these forms:

> It is therefore not unseemly to clothe heavenly things with the veil of the most abject material; for, on the one hand, the material, which derives its existence from Him who in His nature is beautiful, preserves in the order of its parts certain traces of the spiritual Beauty; on the other hand, these very traces enable us to find our way back to the purity of the prototypes, if we are able to discriminate as to how the same model, depending on how one looks on it, can refer either to spiritual or to material things.[19]

It was in Chartres that the doctrine of the Areopagite found its most distinguished exponents; the Cathedral School itself was permeated by his spirit. In Saint-Denis, where, it was believed, the mortal remains of the great master of symbolism lay, his writings must have been read just as eagerly, especially from the beginning of the twelfth century, when contacts with Byzantium revived the study of Greek, which meant that one no longer had to rely solely on the Latin translations of Scotus Eriugena.[20] At any rate, in all of his writings on liturgy and art, Abbot Suger of Saint-Denis shows himself to be the spiritual and intellectual disciple of the Areopagite. Suger however was the builder of the first Gothic church or, if he were not, he was nevertheless the one who made the still completely young Gothic style into the hallmark of the upward-striving Kingdom of France, by employing it for the re-building of the Royal Abbey of Saint-Denis. It is possible that the Archbishop of Sens, Henry the Boar, had built in the Gothic style before him; but Suger's action must have been decisive, for he was the right hand of the King, his counsellor and official.

The re-building of Saint-Denis was for him like the architectural counterpart of his political activity. Suger wrote to the Bishop of Rheims:

> That the glory of the body of Christ, namely the Church, consists of the unity of kingdom and priesthood, is completely clear, because whoever cares for the one also helps the other... the worldly kingdom stands solid through the Church of God, and the Church of God prospers through the worldly kingdom.

The order on earth, as St. Dionysius taught, must resemble as much as possible the order in Heaven, both in the organization of human society and in art; this is the view expressed by Suger, at the beginning of his short book on the construction and consecration of the new Church of Saint-Denis, in the following remarkably subtle words:

> The wonderful power of one single lofty principle compensates the antithesis between human and Godly things by a proper uniting of them, so that apparently contradictory realities—of various kinds and differing origins—are linked by the blessed unison of a superior harmony.[21]

Suger compares the universe to perfect music, in which every dissonance is finally overcome, and he also looks on it as a well-constructed building which in all its parts conforms to the one divine principle or prototype. In such views there is more than a poetic metaphor; they express a certain vision of the world as the art of God, something which we will repeatedly find in the Gothic style, and which continues a Pythagorean heritage in the Christian spirit. Suger continues:

> Those who strive to be illumined through their participation in the highest and eternal principle are always mindful to reconcile like with unlike and to make smooth the mutual conflict of things, as if their penetrating discernment sat on a judge's seat.

In thinking thus he was more statesman than builder, for he strove to unite Church and state in one comprehensive order, by increasing the power of the king as protector of the Church and the poor, while at the same time removing from this power the taint of arbitrary violence. Managing worldly power without betraying Christian teaching is possible only to the one who does not let himself be seduced, and Suger writes thus of the men whom he himself took as examples:

> With the help of the divine mercy, they draw from the source of eternal wisdom the means whereby they may resist inner dissension and uproar, and this they do by preferring the spiritual to the material and the eternal to the ephemeral.

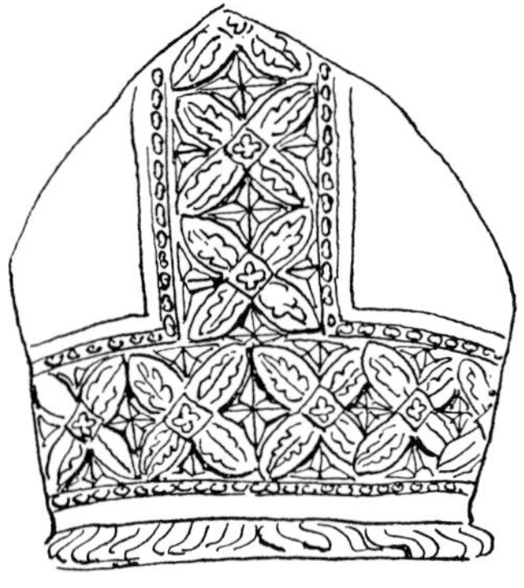

Bishop's mitre from a statue in Chartres cathedral; fragment in the cathedral museum.

The last quoted words seem to have been taken from St. Bernard of Clairvaux. Suger was his friend and in many things his ally. In a certain sense, however, he was also his opponent; for whereas St. Bernard opposed the introduction of splendour into monastic communities, Suger, for spiritual as well as for political reasons, did all he could to make his abbey-church as splendid as possible. St. Bernard writes:

> O vanity of vanities! The Church is resplendent, but the poor go hungry! The walls of churches are covered with gold, while the children of the Church remain naked. Tell me, O poor monks—if indeed ye are still poor—what does gold have to do with a holy place? Frankly speaking, it is covetousness that brings about all this, covetousness, the slave of idols . . . for the sight of splendid and surprising vanities moves men more to giving than to praying. Riches attract riches, just as money attracts money. . . . One blinds the eyes when one provides golden lids for covering relics; the money boxes open! One fashions men and women saints in beautiful forms, and the more worthy of veneration they are the more they are covered with colours! The faithful come in order to kiss them; they are encouraged to give; they see more the beauty of the statues than they venerate the virtues of the saints . . . . The person praying forgets his prayer in viewing them.[22]

To this and similar reproofs, Suger, who himself lived as frugally as a penitent, replied as follows:

> Let everyone act according to his conviction. As for myself, I consider it right that everything that is most precious may serve, especially for the celebration of the most holy Eucharist. If, according to the word of God and at the command of the prophet, golden vessels, golden vials and small golden mortars were used to collect the 'blood of goats, calves and the red heifer', how much more should golden vessels, precious stones, and whatever amongst created things is especially valuable, be used to receive the blood of Christ! . . . Our critics assert that a holy mind, a pure heart, and a pious intention suffice for the holy sacrament. That these are indeed the most important requirements is self-evident. But at the same time we maintain that one should also honour God through the outward beauty of the vessels, and that we must on no account honour anything else in the world to the same extent as we do the holy sacrifice.[23]

The ascetical criticism of ecclesiastical art has, in spiritually fruitful times, always led to its revival, rather as the pruning of a tree increases its fruitfulness. There is an increased appreciation that the outward beauty of art is not only justified by the edifying content of the images, but that beauty in itself must have a spiritual value, and that this lies in its 'anagogical' or symbolical, character, which makes of what is earthly a reflection of the Eternal.

Suger refers to this when he compares the precious stones on the sacred vessels on his altar to the spiritual virtues or to the stages in contemplation or the knowledge of God. He writes:

> Often, out of a pure love for our Holy Mother the Church, I regard the various new and old adornments. When I behold how the wonderful cross of St. Eloysius, along with smaller crosses and some incomparable jewelry, stand on the golden altar, I say from the bottom of my heart: 'Every precious stone is Thy garment, the sardonyx, the topaz, the jasper, the chrysolith, the onyx, the beryl, the sapphire, the carbuncle, and the emerald . . . .' Those who know the properties of precious stones realize to their great astonishment that no single one of them is lacking here, except the carbuncle, and that nearly all of them are richly present.
>
> When, in my joy over the beauty of the House of God through the loveliness of the many-coloured jewels, I am withdrawn from outward cares and a worthy meditation leads me, through transposition of the material into the spiritual, to perceive the various holy virtues, it seems to me as if I dwelt in a strange part of the universe, such as exists neither in the mire of the earth nor in the purity of Heaven, and then, with God's grace, it may happen that in anagogical manner, I am raised up from this lower to that higher world.[24]

Suger's Re-building of the Church of Saint-Denis

SUGER, in his *Little Book on the Consecration of the Church of St. Dionysius* writes:

When the glorious and much-praised Dagobert, King of the Franks . . . had fled to the place known as Catulliacus [now known as Saint-Denis], in order to escape from the intolerable anger of his father Chlothar the Great, and had learned by words and actions that the martyrs buried there (who had appeared to him as wondrously beautiful men in snow-white garments) requested his services . . . he commanded . . . that a basilica of royal splendour be erected in honour of the saints. He furnished the church, in which he had incorporated many marble pillars, with an immense number of treasures of gold and silver, and placed on the walls, pillars and arches multi-coloured hangings adorned with gold and pearls, so that the building, brimful of every earthly beauty, might shine with priceless brilliance. The church lacked only one thing: it was not big enough. Not that the King was short of goodwill, but it may well have been that in these times no larger or even equally large church existed, and perhaps also that, in such a relatively small area, the brilliance of the gold and the luminosity of the previous stones fell more brightly and pleasantly on the eyes.

Because of the restrictedness of the space and the growing number of the faithful who flocked to pray for the saints' intercession, the basilica underwent much stress. On Feast days especially, when the church was already overfilled, large crowds pressing on all the doors had to be turned away. Not only were those demanding entrance denied entry, but the crowds who had succeeded in getting in could not get out. It was sometimes remarkable how those who streamed inside to kiss and venerate the holy relics (the nails and the crown of thorns of Our Lord) reacted to the resistance of the tightly-packed crowd; not being able, cooped up in a crowd of thousands, to move a foot, they stood there as if changed into stone, and knew not if they could still cry out. For women this intolerable pressure was especially painful. Wedged between large men as if in a vice, they fainted out of fear of death, or cried out as if in childbirth. Some of them, who were trampled upon, were, thanks to the excellent presence of mind of some men, lifted up above the heads of the people, and could then walk on them as if on the ground. Many, however, in the courtyard of the brothers, gasping in despair, gave up the ghost. Even the brothers, who showed the crowds the relics of the Passion of Our Lord, were exposed to the pressure and the pushing, and often fled through the windows with their relics, since they had no other means of escape. I heard about all this when I was a schoolboy with the Brothers; as a youth I suffered from it, and when I became a man, my burning desire was to improve the situation.

Around the year 1132 Suger began the re-building:

> Since the narrow ante-chamber (on the north end of the outer front) serving the main entrance was limited on both sides by towers, which were neither high nor especially distinguished and were already close to crumbling, we, fortified with God's support, began the work at this point, after we had laid very strong stone ground-walls for the large nave (enclosed by two towers), and a no less strong spiritual foundation, according to the words: 'No one can lay a foundation other than the one that was laid by and is Jesus Christ.'

At a certain distance from the existing basilica, the construction of which he attributed to King Dagobert, but which in reality originated in the Carolingian

The west front of the Abbey Church of Saint-Denis as it is today.

period, Suger had a new west front built, with two large towers which, along with the intervening elements, he united into an enclosed unit. Through the three doors of the west façade one entered into an antechamber consisting of a nave with two side aisles, above which a second storey contained three chapels. In the Carolingian period, there had been, for the sake of architectural unity, similar west front construction. What is unique to the new building is only the fact that all inner space is covered in with Gothic vaulting.

Suger's façade, which was damaged at the time of the French Revolution and re-worked in the nineteenth century, still looked predominantly Romanesque. And yet the three-fold doorway, whose arches sweep from supporting pillar to supporting pillar, as well as the weightless breadth of the windows, already announced the open countenance of the Gothic church façade. This west front construction is still half intended for defence – Suger himself said that in case of need the spires could be used for defence – but still more is it an image of the celestial door of triumph.

The west front of the Abbey Church of Saint-Denis, after the artistic reconstruction by S. M. K. Crosby.

This is emphasized especially by the rose windows, which here, perhaps for the first time, adorn the front of a church with their sun-like presence. Suger did not invent them; he merely accorded them the dominant role which thenceforward they were to play. As an architectural form, they derive, like many other elements of the Gothic style – the pointed arch, the rib-vaulting, the tracery – from Islamic art; their nearest model is to be found in the round windows, filled with a lattice-work of stone or stucco, of certain Mozarabic churches (that is, the churches of the Christian communities in Moorish Spain). In Christian architecture, the round wheel-like window took on the role of the similarly wheel-like 'monogram of Christ', which formerly adorned Syrian, Byzantine, and Romanesque doorfronts; this monogram device was later displaced by figurative sculpture, but it reappeared, in architectural form, in the rose windows. From early times, every wheel-shaped device had associated a Christological interpretation with the symbolism of the world wheel, and this dual significance was also present in the pictorial decoration of the Gothic rose windows; it had already appeared in the stone sculptures which sometimes surrounded the rose windows. Occasionally it is the four animals of the Apocalypse that surround the halo of the *majestas Domini*; at other times, circularly ascending and descending figures turn the rose window into a wheel of fortune, which, for its part, as wheel of fate, represents a form of the world wheel.

Rose window from the Church of San Miguel de Sillo, near Naranco (Oviedo, Spain), ninth century.

Who was the architect who realized Suger's plans? We do not know, nor do we know to what extent he could proceed on his own; for Suger seems to have involved himself intimately, not only with the spiritual idea, but also with technical questions. He writes:

> With God's help, we discovered a new quarry, of the highest quality, and of a richness and productiveness that had never before been seen in our area. Also, a large number of skilled bricklayers, stonemasons, sculptors and other craftsmen became available. Thus divine providence freed us from cares of all kinds, by providing us with unexpected help .... Solomon's riches would have availed him no more than ours, had not the same Author, with regard to the same work, generously stood by His servants. The unity of Author and work is the builder's sufficiency.

The wall-supports of the three doors, as well as the tympanums and arched surrounds, were all decorated with figures, of which today only nineteenth-century reproductions remain in place. In the tympanum of the central door, the Last Judgement was represented, just as at Beaulieu and Conques. The doors were of gilded bronze:

> After we had summoned bronze-founders and chosen sculptors, the main door was constructed, on which the Passion of Our Lord and His Resurrection, as well as His Ascension, were represented, with a great amount of gilding, as was seemly for such a noble door.

The inscription which Suger caused to be written on the main doorway was as follows:

> Whoever thou mayst be, who art minded to praise this door,
> Wonder not at the gold, nor at the cost, but at the work.
> The work shines in its nobility; by shining nobly,
> May it illumine the spirit, so that, through its trusty lights,
> The spirit may reach the true Light in which Christ is the Door.
> The golden door proclaims the nature of the Inward:
> Through sensible things, the heavy spirit is raised to the Truth;
> From the depths, it rises to the Light.

These lines recall the words of the Areopagite: 'The higher world casts its light on the lower world, and, in sensible things, is like a trace of purely spiritual things.'

When the west front was completed to the level of the spires, Suger had the idea of joining it to the old nave, which meant extending the pillared arcades of the latter several bays towards the west:

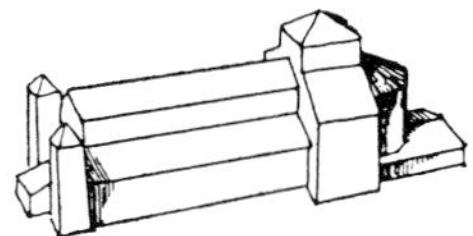

Model reconstruction of the original Carolingian Abbey Church of Saint-Denis.

> Our aim above all was to ensure that the new building be in keeping with the old. By dint of thought, questioning, and enquiries in a number of distant places, we sought to learn where we could obtain marble or equally worthy pillars. Since however we could find them nowhere, it seemed to our anxious minds that there was no other solution than to have them brought from Rome (where we had seen some magnificent pillars in the Diocletian and other baths), by reliable ships through the Mediterranean sea and the English channel, and then to us along the winding River Seine—all this at great expense and by courtesy of our enemies and neighbours the Saracens. We remained many years uninspired, considering and seeking, until suddenly the generosity of the Almighty condescended to still our concern and, through the merits of the holy martyrs, led us to discover what none of us had dared to hope . . . . Near Pontoise, not far from our place, lay an excellent quarry on the slope of a deep valley. This had been excavated, not by nature, but by the industry of men, who for ages past had obtained their mill-stones there. Until now it had yielded nothing extraordinary, but had guarded its treasures, as we believe, for the sake of our great and sacred building, as if they were first fruits for God and the holy martyrs.
>
> Whenever the pillars were dragged up from the lowest part of the slope by means of ropes knotted together, local people and neighbours, nobles and commoners, would humbly convey them further, their

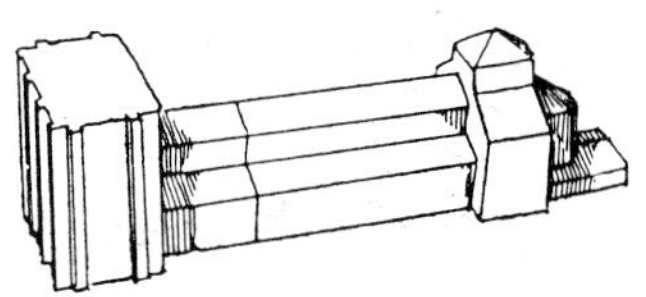

Model of the original Abbey Church of Saint-Denis with Suger's western addition of June 1140.

> bodies and arms harnessed like draught animals. In the steep street in the middle of the village, our men would go out to meet them; they would stop what they were doing and with their own strength would help overcome the difficulties of the way.... A miracle occurred which we ourselves heard from witnesses.... One day when it had become gloomy and dark because of heavy rain, the men who normally loaded the carts going to the quarry had left their work. The ox-drivers began to complain that they were wasting their time as long as the workers were not there. They did not stop complaining until some weak and frail men along with a few boys – seventeen in all and, if I remember correctly, accompanied by a priest – hurried to the quarry, took up a rope, and attached it to one of the pillars.... Moved by pious zeal, the small band prayed: 'St. Dionysius, if it please thee, help us so that for thy sake we may raise this pillar, for thou canst not blame us if we cannot do it alone.' Thereupon, putting all their strength into it, they pulled up, from the depth of the valley, the weight which otherwise a hundred and eighty, or at least a hundred, men could pull only with the greatest effort. They did not do this, however, with their own strength alone, but through the will of God and with the help of the saints whom they had invoked.

When the arcades and the walls of the nave had been extended to the newly built west front, all this had to be covered in. It was the practice of the carpenters to construct in one piece, with strong beams, the base of the triangle formed by the rafters, so that they held together the outer walls like a clamp.

> When in our search for roof timbers we asked our own carpenters and those from Paris for advice, they replied – from their point of view correctly – that in these areas, because of the scarcity of woods, none could be found, but must be obtained from the region of Auxerre. All expressed the same opinion, and so we were very depressed because of the difficulties and waste of time that would be involved in bringing them from there. One night however when I had returned from matins, I lay in bed thinking, and made up my mind personally to visit all parts of our woods and inspect them thoroughly, so that time might be saved if indeed timber could be obtained from them. We abandoned all other duties and in early morning made our way with carpenters and woodfellers to the woods of Iveline. When we reached the Chevreuse valley, we summoned our foresters and labourers who were familiar with the other woods and asked them on their oath whether, irrespective of difficulty, we could find here wood of the necessary size. They smiled in amazement, and would have laughed at us outright if they had dared. They asked if we did not know that in the whole region nothing of the kind could be found, especially Milo, our castle steward at Chevreuse, who with another held half of the woods in tenure from us, and who, for the purpose of building defence towers and bulwarks, would have left no such tree untouched and undamaged.... But we paid no attention to them and, firm in faith, began to walk through the woods where, after an hour, we came upon a tree of sufficient size. And what happened after that? By the ninth hour or earlier, to the astonishment of everyone, especially the locals, we selected, amidst the thorns and

> undergrowth of the dark wood, twelve large trees – exactly the number required. When they had been brought to the sacred basilica, we covered over the building, in the midst of much rejoicing, and to the praise and glory of Our Lord Jesus, who had preserved the beams from the hand of the plunderer, and had kept them for Himself and the holy martyrs. Thus in this work was manifested the Divine Goodness, which determines everything 'in weight and measure', neither too much nor too little; for it was exactly the required amount of wood, and no further tree was found.

In June of 1140 the new west front and its connection with the old nave was consecrated jointly by the Bishops of Rouen, Beauvais and Senlis. Now Suger turned to a new task: he postponed the further building of the west towers and began to create from an entirely new start the most important part of the church, the choir. The existing choir was demolished, and the stones from it (which according to legend had been consecrated by Christ Himself) were preserved as relics with a view to their being incorporated in the new choir. The roof of the crypt, which lay under the choir, had to be raised

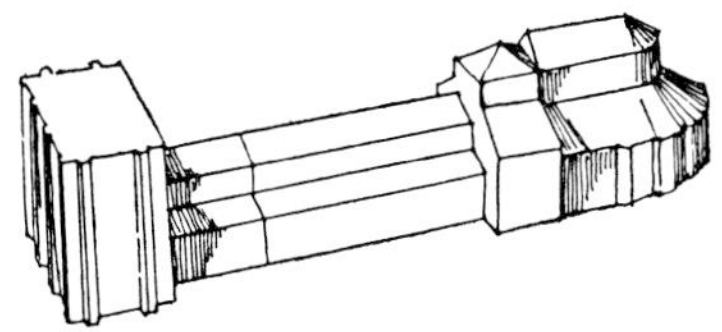

The Abbey Church of St. Denis with the original central building, the uncompleted western addition of Suger, and the new choir.

> so that it might serve as a floor for those who would walk on the steps now constructed on both sides. In this way the shrines of the saints, decorated with gold and the costliest of precious stones, would most effectively meet their regard.

A special problem arose from the fact that the pillars of the new ambulatory had to be placed over the crypt and, at the same time, brought into unison with the breadth of the central nave and the two aisles. In this way the pillars of the crypt would not be seen from the nave. The problem, in Suger's words, was solved by 'geometric and arithmetic means'. This meant that the architect commissioned by Suger was able to bring the arrangement of the pillars of both choir and nave into the common denominator of a basic geometrical form, in a way that corresponded to the ideal of medieval architecture. What this basic form was can no longer be

Groundplan of the Abbey Church of St. Denis at the time of Suger, showing the various building phases; after Erwin Panofsky.

Original Carolingian building

The foundations of the walls of the Carolingian west front replaced by Suger

Carolingian crypt

Suger's additions

Junction of Suger's additions with the original basilica

A = Reliquary in the choir

B = High altar

C = Monks' choir

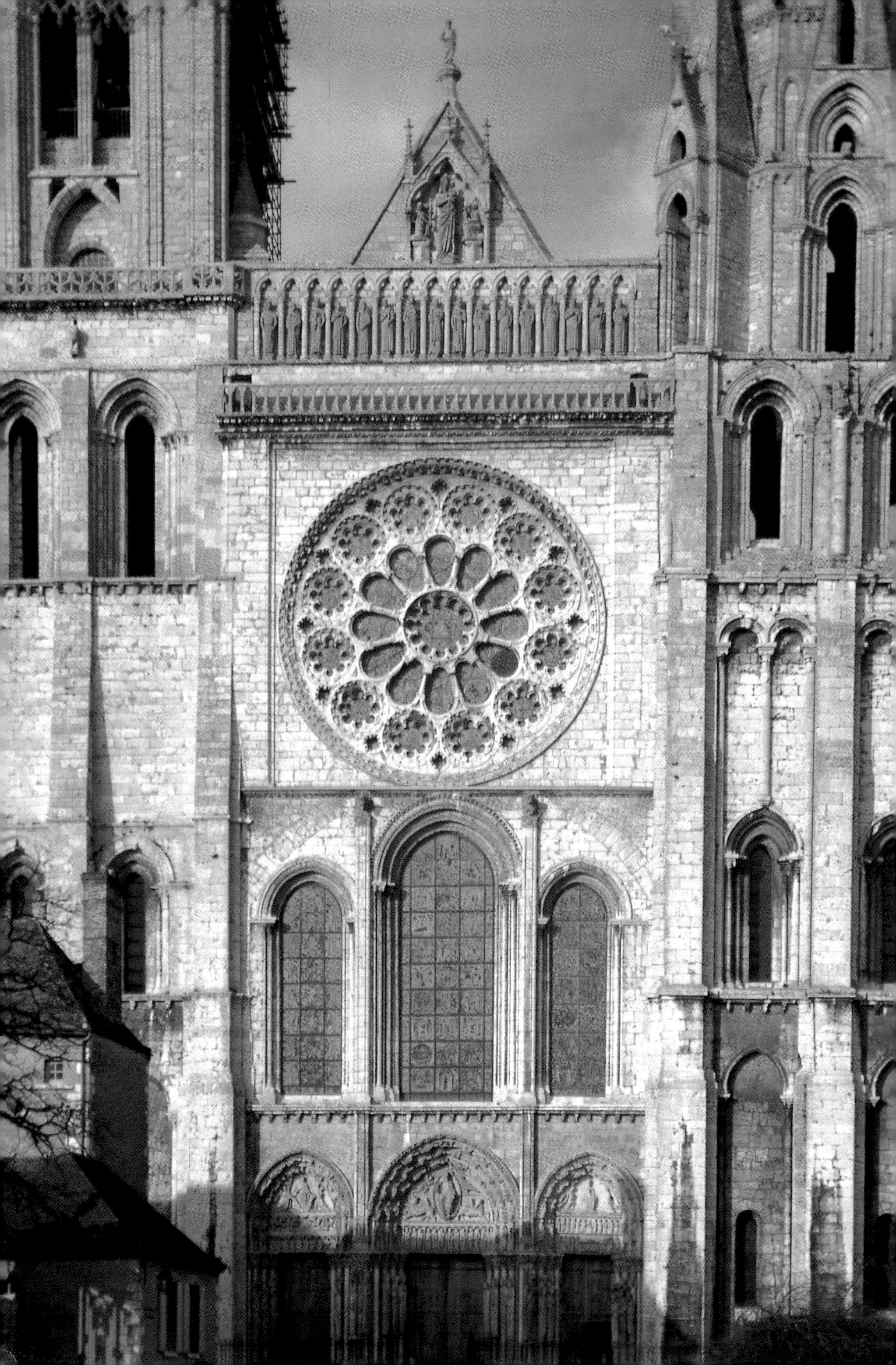

Artist's impression of Suger's choir and the lower part of the earlier choir (darker shading) with the Carolingian crypt; after Erwin Panofsky.

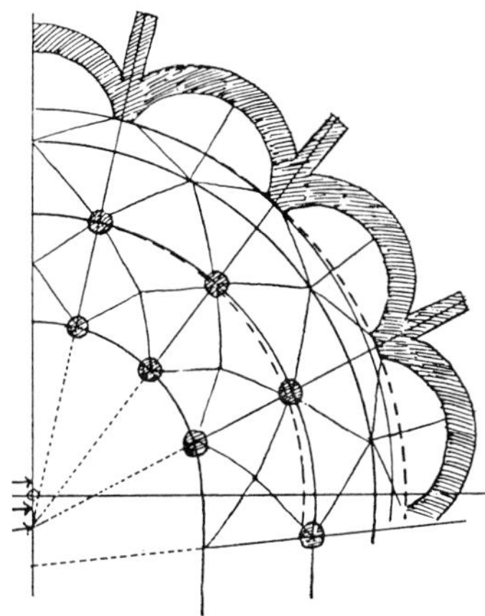

Scheme of Suger's choir, after Viollet-le-Duc: the main circles of the double ambulatory are not concentric; neither do the radii, which separate the chapels, meet in the centre of the innermost semi-circle. These departures from geometric unity ensure that the breadths of the individual vaults be similar to one another and also that one can have a better view into the garland of chapels from the nave.

determined with certainty from the existing building, which subsequently underwent many alterations. One thing, however, does emerge when one looks at the still unaltered arrangement of the pillars in the choir itself: the radial divisions of the choir do not radiate outwards from the exact centre of the innermost half circle, but take the form of a folded fan. This may well have been with a view to making the garland of choir chapels more visible from the nave than a strictly radial arrangement would have done.

As soon as the plan was decided upon, and the trenches were dug for the foundation walls of the choir, Suger gathered together 'a goodly number of distinguished men, including bishops and abbots', and also requested the presence of the King of the Franks, Louis VII:

> On Sunday, the day before the Ides of July, we organized a grand procession, with many distinguished personalities. At the head of everything, in the hands of the Bishops and Abbots, were carried the instruments of the Passion of Our Lord, the nails and the crown of thorns, as well as the arm of the holy elder Simeon and other relics. With humble and devoted hearts, we stepped down into the ditches which had been dug to take the foundations. We entreated the assistance of the Holy Spirit, that He would bring the auspiciously begun House of God to a good end, and, singing the praises of God and solemnly chanting the Psalm 'It is founded on the holy mountain', we laid the foundation stones, after the bishops had, with their own hands, prepared the mortar with the holy water of the previous consecration on the 9th June. Our noble king himself stepped down and laid a stone with his own hands; thereupon we ourselves and many other abbots and ecclesiastics laid stones. Many also included precious stones out of love and veneration for Jesus Christ, and sang: 'Precious stones are all Thy walls.'

Facing page
The west front of Chartres cathedral.

For three years, at great expense and with the help of many craftsmen, we pursued the completion of the work, so that God could not with justice reproach us. The middle of the building was raised, borne by twelve pillars, corresponding to the number of the twelve Apostles, and also by the same number of pillars in the aisles, representing the numbers of the Prophets, according to the words of the Apostle (who does his building in the spirit): 'Be no longer guests and foreigners, but citizens with the saints and God's house-companions'; build on the ground of the Apostles and Prophets, for Jesus Christ is the cornerstone, in Whom every building, be it material or spiritual, 'grows into a sacred temple in the Lord', and in whom we ourselves should be united. For the more we are united spiritually, the better and more freely we will succeed in building materially.

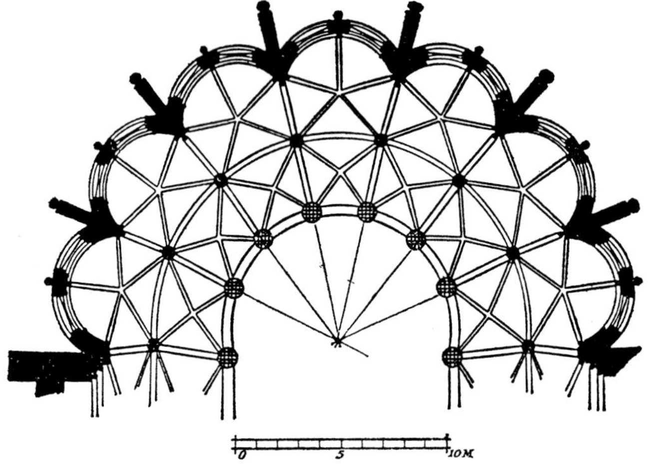

Suger's choir at St. Denis.

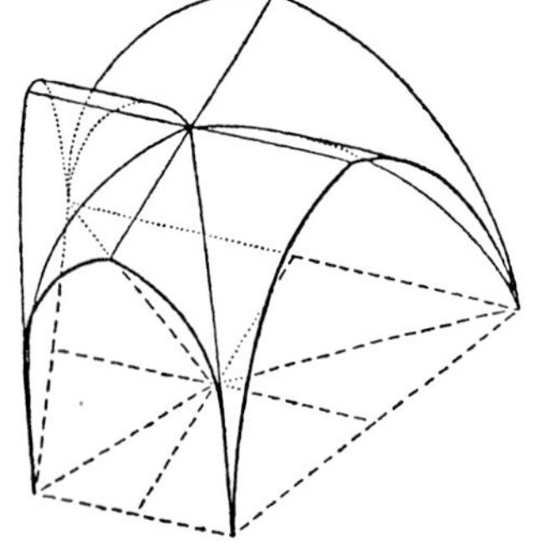

Spatial representation of a single vault of a Gothic choir ambulatory; after John Fitchen.

The Gothic choir of Saint-Denis, in the regularity and lightness of its arrangement, has not been surpassed by any later choir. Not a single piece of wall in it is superfluous. Round the inner ambulatory there is a second, outer, one, which consists of seven chapels that give onto the transparent shell. Suger himself speaks of the 'elegant and excellently planned garland of chapels, through which the whole sanctuary is filled with wonderful and unbroken light.'

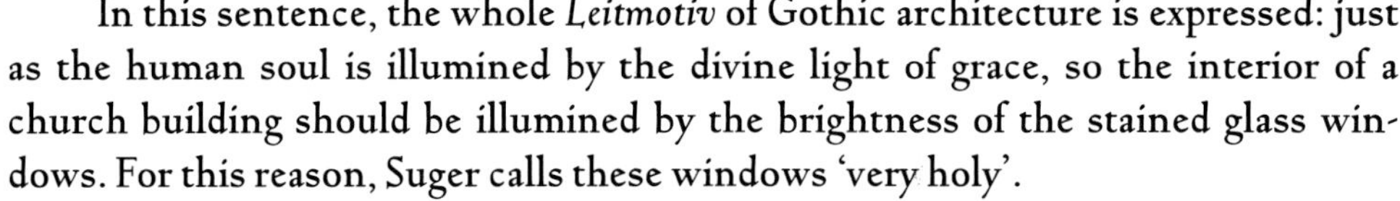

In this sentence, the whole *Leitmotiv* of Gothic architecture is expressed: just as the human soul is illumined by the divine light of grace, so the interior of a church building should be illumined by the brightness of the stained glass windows. For this reason, Suger calls these windows 'very holy'.

The illuminating effect of the stained glass windows would be impossible without Gothic vaulting, which makes available the whole extent of the wall, right up to the roof. The Gothic art of vaulting, however, requires that the structure of arches and ribs be first constructed, before the shell of the vault is built over them. Both the barrel vaulting and cross vaulting of Romanesque architecture could be constructed on appropriately shaped wooden formwork. As the masonry dried and set, one had only gradually to remove the supporting formwork. In the case, however, of the multiple curvatures of Gothic vaulting (which are not reducible to simple forms), and especially in the case of a garland of vaulting as in the choir of Saint-Denis, this procedure is not possible. Consequently the arches and ribs had first to be built and, to help do this, wooden scaffolding was used. Only when the stone skeleton was ready, the mortar having finally set and the scaffolding having

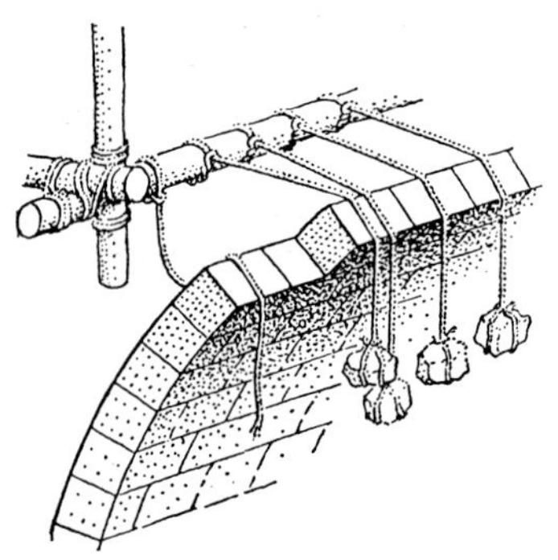

Method of closing a vault without wooden framework; after John Fitchen.

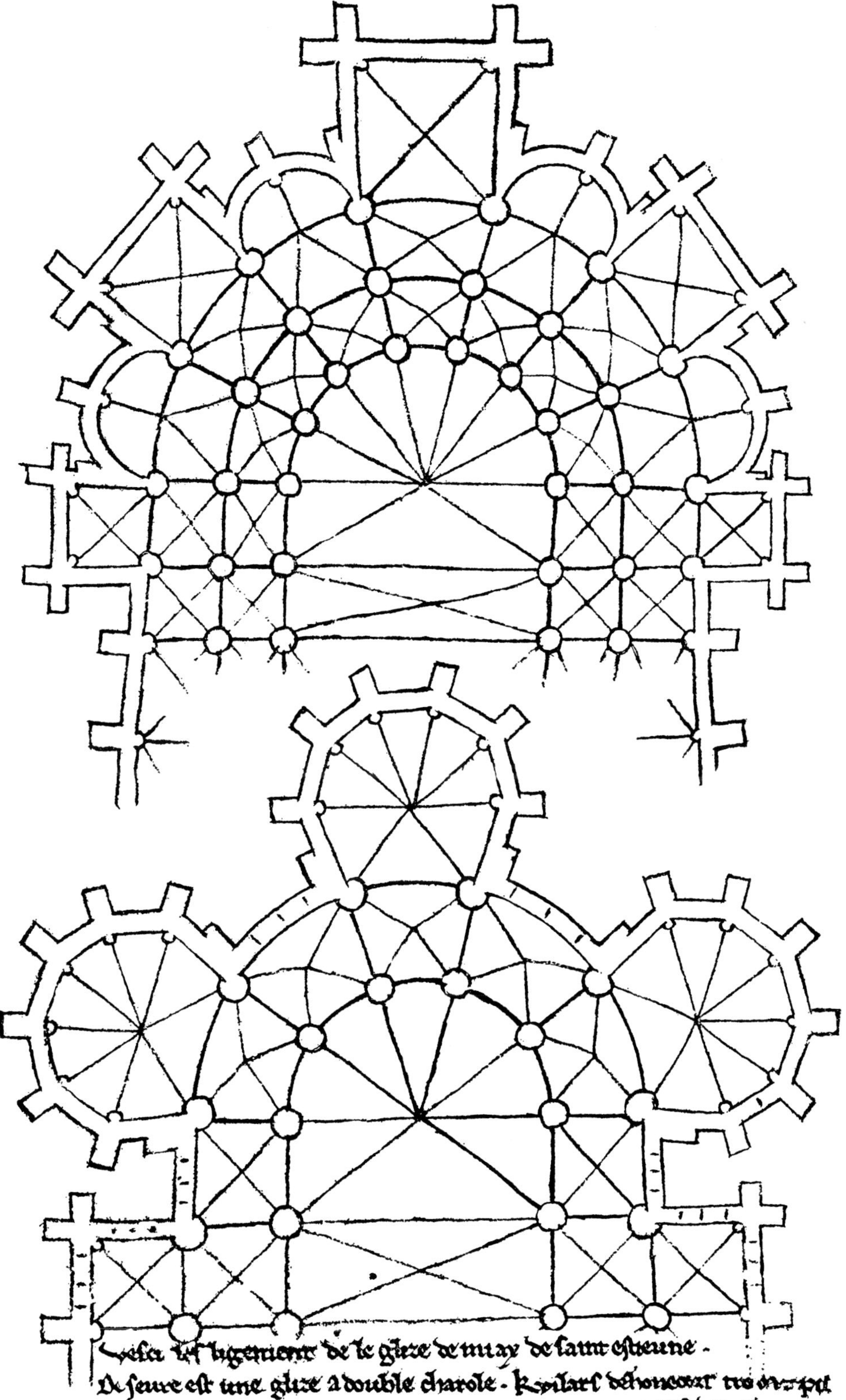

Outlines of two choirs, from the sketchbook of Villard de Honnecourt, who comments: 'Here is the plan of Saint-Etienne-de-Meaux. Above is a church with a double choir ambulatory, as found by Villard de Honnecourt and Pierre de Corbie.' These choirs, surrounded by many chapels, obviously gave much less light to the interior of the church than did the choir built by Suger at St. Denis.

been removed, could the vault coverings be laid on, or rather, between the arches and ribs. This could be done simply by the naked eye, and without formwork. The stones that projected over the centre of gravity were temporarily held in place by ropes tensioned by weights.

In Suger's day, this method of construction must have been completely new. And it immediately had to face a hard test:

Just as the new building, with its capitals and upper arches, was being raised to its crown, and the main arches still stood free and not yet joined together by the intercalated shells, a dreadful and almost unbearable storm broke out, the skies darkened, and the rain poured down. The storm blew so fiercely that solid houses, even stone towers, and wooden defence structures, were made to reel. The storm occurred on the remembrance day (19th January) of the renowned King Dagobert; His Lordship Bishop Geoffroy of Chartres was solemnly celebrating mass on the main altar for the repose of his soul, when the immense power of the storm caught the arches, which were not supported by scaffolding nor held fast by any supporting building. Shaking piteously, they rocked to and fro, and threatened to fall down. When the Bishop saw with horror that the arches and their rafters were beginning to totter, he several times stretched out his hand of blessing towards them and, entreatingly, proffered the arm of St. Simeon, at the same time making the sign of the cross, so that apparently, not his spiritual power, but solely God's benevolence and the merit of the saints prevented the arches from falling. Thus the storm, which in many places brought disaster by destroying solid buildings, was warded off by divine intervention, and the recently built and as yet unbounded arches were saved from destruction.

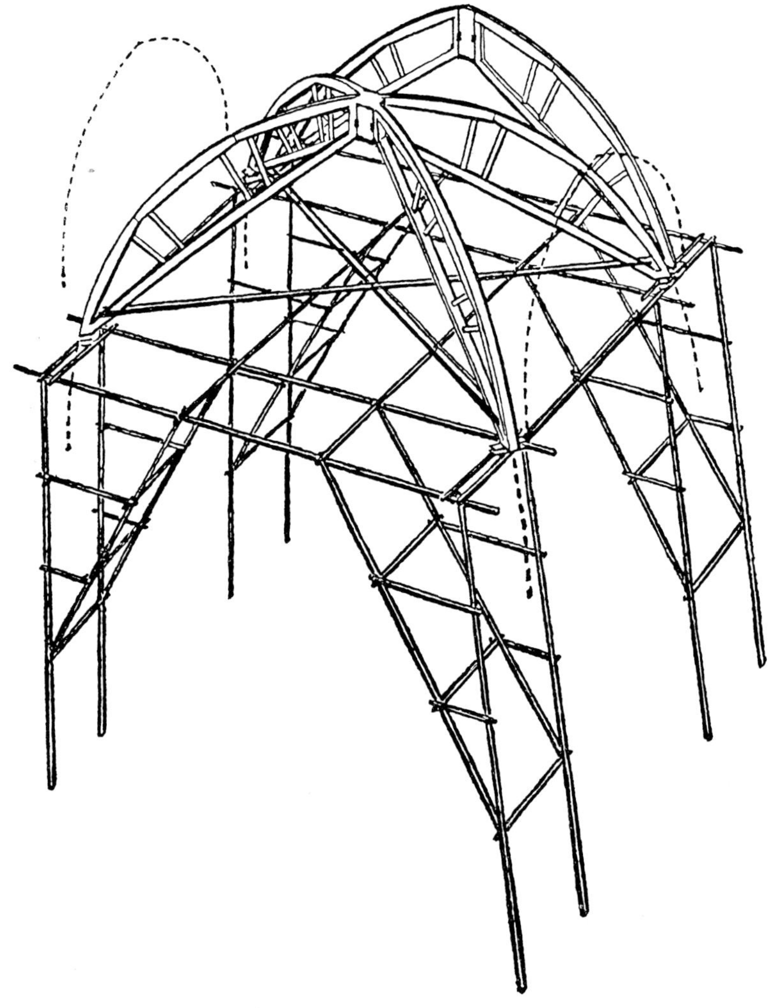

Scaffolding for the ribs of a Gothic vault; after John Fitchen.

Facing page
One of the stained-glass windows of the west wall of Chartres cathedral, representing the human genealogy of Christ in the form of a tree which springs from the loins of Jesse and grows through the Royal House of David to reach its flowering in Christ, situated immediately above the Virgin Mary. On the right and left of the tree are the Prophets who foretold the birth of Christ. The window is a faithful reproduction of a similar stained-glass window—ordered by Suger for his abbatial church—of which only a part now remains, and which portrayed this symbolical composition for the first time.

On the second Sunday of June 1144 the new choir was due to be consecrated:

> We sent out invitations by many messengers, couriers, and ambassadors to almost all regions of France and strongly requested the archbishops and bishops to be present at this great feast.... Our Lord King Louis himself, his consort Queen Eleanor, his mother and the peers of the realm arrived on the third day. Innumerable were the counts and nobles from many regions and districts, as well as the usual companies of knights and soldiers. I should like, however, to name the archbishops and bishops who were present: Samson, Archbishop of Rheims; Hugues, Archbishop of Rouen; Guy, Archbishop of Sens; Theobald, Archbishop of Canterbury; Jocelin, Bishop of Soissons; Simon, Bishop of Noyon; Elias, Bishop of Orléans; Eudes, Bishop of Beauvais; Hugues, Bishop of Auxerre; Alvise, Bishop of Arras; Guy, Bishop of Châlons; Algare, Bishop of Coutances; Rotrou, Bishop of Evreux; Milon, Bishop of Térouanne; Manasse, Bishop of Meaux; Pierre, Bishop of Senlis....

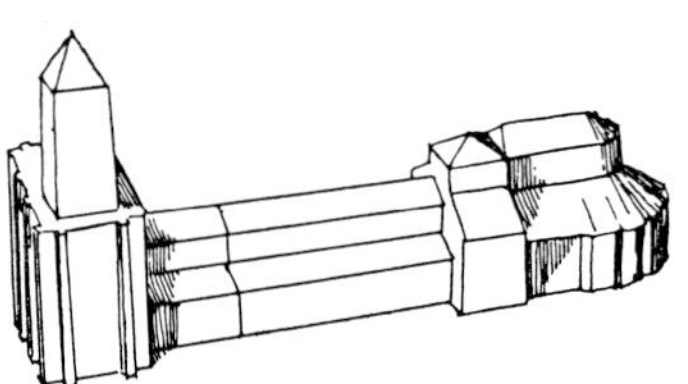

Model of the Abbey Church of St. Denis as it was around 1148.

In this gathering, the builders of the very first Gothic cathedrals were represented: the Cathedral of Sens was then under construction; and those of Noyon and Senlis were due to be started soon after 1150 by the two bishops named by Suger. In Chartres, work was proceeding on the Royal Door on the west façade. The Gothic cathedrals of Laon, Paris, Canterbury, Meaux, Soissons, Rheims, Beauvais, Auxerre, Châlons, Evreux, and Orléans were all to be built under the next generation of bishops.

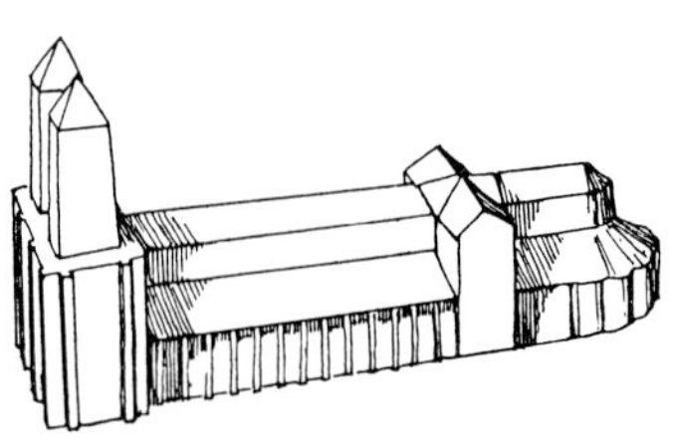

Model of the definitive form of St. Denis as planned by Suger, but not completely achieved by him, after S. M. K. Crosby.

> After we had spent the whole night reciting matins in praise of God, we humbly entreated our Lord Jesus Christ, the Intercessor for our sins, that He... might graciously descend... and participate in the ceremonies, not only in His power, but in His own Person. In the early morning, te archbishops and the bishops, along with their archdeacons, abbots, and other worthy persons, came from their various inns to the church, dressed themselves in their episcopal garments, and solemnly took their places near the holy water stoup in the upper choir, between the tombs of the saints and the altar of the Saviour. O had ye but seen—for those present could not look on it without deep emotion—how this great choir of high priestly dignitaries in white garments, crowned in white mitres trimmed with gold-ornamented borders, holding their shepherd's crooks in their hands, walked in procession around the holy water basin and invoked the Name of God to drive away evil spirits. Had ye but seen how reverently these famous and admirable men celebrated the wedding of the Eternal Bridegroom, such that the king and the assembled nobility could have sworn that they beheld a heavenly and not an earthly choir, and that they were present, not at a human, but at a divine ceremony! The crowd of the faithful circled round the building in an unbearable throng, and when the choir of bishops, according to custom, sprinkled the outer walls with holy water, the king himself, with his officers, held back the pressure of the crowd and protected those who, with shepherd's crooks and candles, tried to return to the door.

The medieval liturgist Durand de Mende describes the rite of church consecration as follows:

> After everyone, except one single deacon, has left the [newly built] church, the Bishop, who with the clergy is standing in front of the door, blesses the water, to which salt has been added. During this time, twelve candles burn inside the church in front of the twelve painted crosses on the church wall. Then the clergy, accompanied by the people, walk round the outer walls of the church, and sprinkle it from a bundle of hyssop with holy water. Having again reached the door of the church, the Bishop knocks on it with his shepherd's crook and says: 'Ye princes, open your doors, ye eternal gates, lift yourselves up, and the King of Glory will make His entry.' To this, the deacon inside replies: 'Who is this King of Glory?' And the Pontifex replies: 'The Lord is strong and powerful, the Lord is a hero in battle.' After the circumambulation of the church and the knocking at the door has been performed three times, the door is opened, and the Bishop makes his entry with a small group of ministrants, while the remaining clergy and the people remain outside. The Bishop greets the church with the words: 'Peace be upon this house!' Then he recites litanies. A cross is then drawn on the floor of the church (diagonally to the main axes) with ashes and sand, in which the whole alphabet, in Greek and Latin letters, is inscribed. Once again the Bishop blesses water, salt, ashes and wine, and consecrates the altar. Finally he anoints with oil the twelve painted crosses on the wall.

Regarding the meaning of the procedure, Durand writes:

> Everything which is here performed visibly, evokes God in the soul invisibly, for the soul is the temple of the true God.... The church to be consecrated is none other than the soul, which must be sanctified....
>
> The threefold circumambulation of the church by the Bishop signifies the threefold coming of Christ: His descent into the world, His descent into hell, and His resurrection.
>
> The writing of the alphabet [in Greek and Latin] represents the Testaments, both of which are fulfilled by the Cross of Christ....

The diagonal cross of ash, in which the two alphabets are inscribed, resembles, as Adhémar of Chabannes[25] points out, the Greek letter 'Chi' (X), the initial letter of 'Christos', which is here related to the axial cross of the sacred building 'like a wheel within a wheel', as Durand says.

After the church was consecrated, the relics of the martyrs, which had temporarily been housed in tents outside the church, had to be brought to their new home in the raised choir. While the bishops made their way to the opened shrines, Suger invited the young King himself to carry the bones of St. Dionysius into the newly built sanctuary. Thereupon

> our Lord the King entered into the throne of bishops and received from their hands the silver shrine of our unique Patron Saint—I think from the hands of the Archbishops of Rheims and Sens and the Bishop of Chartres and others—and led the crowd with such pious and noble bearing. O wonder to behold! No one has ever seen such a procession!

O how the bodies of the holy martyrs and witnesses were brought out of the tents, on the shoulders of the bishops, counts and barons, in order to meet the most holy Dionysius and his companions! – O how the procession, with candles, crosses, and other solemn ornaments, singing hymns and odes, passed through the transept! – O how the men, lovingly and weeping with joy, carried their Patron Saint! No greater joy can ever have overcome them on this earth.

On entering a newly built church, the hymn *Urbs Jerusalem beata* was sung:

> Blessed city of Jerusalem, known as vision of peace,
> Built in Heaven of living stones,
> Decorated with angels, like a noble bride.
>
> Once more thou descendest from Heaven,
> Prepared for the bridal covenant with the Lord,
> Thy walls and roofs are of pure gold.
>
> Thy doors stand open, shining with pearls
> And the brightness of virtues; they permit entry to all those
> Who, for Christ's Name's sake, have suffered oppression.
>
> Polished smooth by affliction,
> The stones are now ready, and are inserted
> Into the sacred building by the craftsmen's skilful hand.[26]

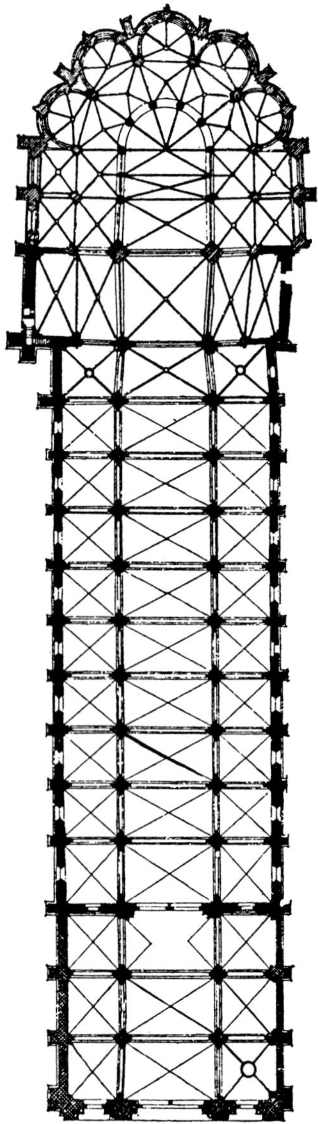

Groundplan of the Abbey Church of St. Mary Magdalene at Vézelay.

Facing page. The Romanesque abbatial church of St. Mary Magdalene at Vézelay in Burgundy has an early Gothic choir, which showers light on the Romanesque nave, rather in the manner of the choir at Saint-Denis, which probably was its model. The choir fits in with the Romanesque structure without any clash or contradiction, but nevertheless with a definite change of mood, a sort of transition to a lighter and brighter world. The Romanesque basilica itself, with its blissful peacefulness and clarity, represents a highpoint of medieval architecture. Though thoroughly Romanesque, it nevertheless approximates to the Gothic ideal through its luminous breadth. Its cross-vaulting was as finely stretched as was possible without buttresses, to the extent that it risked collapsing, and later had to be supported from outside. As in the mature Gothic cathedrals, the arches of the nave and of the aisles keep in step with one another, so that on the top of the nave, they appear almost flat. The Romanesque nave was built between 1120 and 1140, and the Gothic choir towards the end of the twelfth century. It allows us to have an accurate idea of how Suger's choir at Saint-Denis must have looked.

Hard Labour for God

IN JUNE 1144, Suger consecrated his new church; the following year, St. Bernard preached the second crusade; and, in the same year, the so-called 'hard labour for God' originated and spread: young and old, rich and poor, applied their shoulders to carts and wagons, in order to convey to the site whatever was necessary for the building of the church. The chronicler Robert de Torigny writes:

> It happened for the first time at Chartres that people with their own shoulders pulled heavy carts full of stones, wood, sand, and other things necessary for the building of the cathedral, the towers of which sprang up forthwith. Whoever has not seen this, will never see anything like it. And not only in Chartres, but throughout the whole of France, in Normandy and many other places, people humbled themselves, did penance with sorrow and contrition, and forgave their enemies. One saw men and women, sinking up to their knees, drag carts through quagmires, one saw how they laid themselves open to strokes of the discipline, how everywhere miracles occurred, and how God was praised for this with singing and rejoicing.[27]

In all of this, various currents flowed together and formed a new or reawakened cult of the Holy Virgin: the longing for the Holy Land, the true home, the need to turn to the maternal mercy of God, and the chivalric cult of the celestial Lady as the epitome of nobility of soul, innocence and beauty. St. Bernard himself, who knew how to call forth the highest spiritual powers of his contemporaries, is said to have been the first to use the chivalric mode of address *notre Dame* ('Our Lady') for the Mother of God. Not for nothing does many a Gothic cathedral bear this name.

The Church—*ecclesia*—had always been compared to the Holy Virgin. However, at the time when the Gothic style appeared, this viewpoint came into prominence and began to determine the nature of church building: the City of God or the House of the Lord had to be the paradisal palace of the Virgin, or indeed her very image.

Chartres was the centre of the new cult of Mary, for its cathedral was looked on as the principal sanctuary of the Mother of God in France. Its origin was traced back to Celtic times: according to a tradition which is mentioned in the 'old chronicle' of the cathedral, the Druids already venerated, in the spring-grotto over which the cathedral stands, a 'virgin who will give birth'. Until the French Revolution, a primitive statue, carved out of pear wood, of a maternal figure with a child on her lap, was conserved in Chartres. It is not known whether this was a Gallo-Roman carving or a medieval reproduction thereof. The legend in itself is not improbable, since almost all the peoples of antiquity recognized a feminine aspect of the Divinity, which as the generative principle of all things is not only maternal, but also, in her immutable essence, eternally virgin.

In the holy mass, the priests of Chartres prayed: 'O Lord, may this city of Chartres, to which more than all others in Gaul Thou hast revealed the secret of Thine Incarnation, be transformed into the Heavenly Jerusalem.'[28]

As pledge of divine grace, the pilgrims who came to Chartres, venerated the *sancta camisia*, the tunic of the Blessed Virgin, which Charlemagne had brought from Byzantium to Aachen, and which Charles the Bald, in the year 876, presented to the church at Chartres. It has the form of a simple rectangular piece of silk.

In 1134, the west front of the Romanesque cathedral at Chartres fell victim to fire. Bishop Geoffroy de Lèves, a friend of Suger and Bernard of Clairvaux, undertook the building of a new west front flanked with two towers. A start was immediately made with the northern tower and then, in 1145, with the southern. The magnificent Royal Door between the two towers was also under construction during this period.

Archbishop Hugo of Rouen (who was present at the consecration of Saint-Denis) wrote to Bishop Thierry of Amiens as follows:

> It was in Chartres that people began humbly to pull carts and wagons in order to help with the building of the church, and their humility was rewarded with shining miracles. Reports thereof quickly spread everywhere and even awakened our own Normandy. The people in our diocese, after they had received our blessing, also made their way there in order to make good their votive offering. They returned with the resolution to imitate the people of Chartres. They made it a rule for themselves that no one would be received into their community before he had been to confession and had carried out the prescribed penance. Anyone who wished to join them had to renounce anger and malice and to reconcile himself with his enemies in agreement and peace. Those thus united would choose one of their number to be their leader, on whose orders, in humility and silence, they would pull the carts with their own shoulders.[29]

It was striking to see how the people spontaneously linked the movement (which had freely arisen) to spiritual criteria which alone validate a sacrifice. The Bishop of Rouen goes on:

> These three things, namely, confession and penance, the forgiving of enemies, and humility with obedience, we impose as a condition on all those who come to us [in order to obtain our authorization for the 'service of God with carts']. If they fulfil these conditions, we receive them benevolently and give them our blessing. If they then give themselves over to the way with the right attitude, it often happens that their faith is rewarded with miracles, which God, in our church, works on the sick that they bring with them, so that they recover their health.

In the same year 1145, the Abbot Haimo of Saint-Pierre-sur-Dive wrote in a letter to his confrères in Tutbury:

> Whoever saw anywhere, whoever heard in previous generations of tyrants, princes, the powerful in this world, bloated with honours and riches, noblemen and noblewomen, bending their proud and haughty necks under the harness of carts, in order to bring to Christ's refuge, like draught animals, wine, corn, oil, lime, stones, wood and many other things necessary for the feeding of the building workers and the construction of the church? It is remarkable to observe that, during this work, even when thousands of men and women are involved (for the materials to be moved are so massive, the vehicles so bulky, and the

loads thereon so heavy), a complete silence reigns, and not a single word nor the slightest murmuring can be heard. If one had not seen it with one's own eyes, it would be impossible to believe that such a great number were present. If there be a rest pause on the way, no sound is heard except for confessions of sins, supplications, and pure prayers to God, that He may forgive sins. As priests pray, all hatred is silenced and all discord left aside, all debts are settled and the unity of souls restored. Should there be one among them whose heart is too hardened for him to forgive his enemies, or who harkens not to the pious exhortations of the priest, his sacrifice is rejected as impure. He is cast out of the community of the holy people in shame and disgrace. When the faithful people, to the sound of trumpets and bearing sacred standards, have set out on the way, nothing they encounter can stop them, neither high mountains nor deep waters; you would think that you beheld the ancient Hebrew people crossing the Jordan in multitudes. When our pilgrims have to cross some stream or river, they wade in with such confidence that the Lord Himself seems to lead them. Even the waves of the sea restrained themselves to enable them to come to us; this miracle occurred at Sainte-Marie-du-Port, and eyewitnesses told us about it.

Having reached the church which they wish to help build, they erect around themselves a sort of field camp, and during the whole night following their arrival, the army of the Lord keep vigil and sing psalms and hymns. On each of the wagons candles and lamps are lit. The ill and the fragile are placed on the wagons. In order to bring them relief, the relics of the saints are carried past, and prayers are said for them. Then processions are held, with priests and clerics leading and the people following; with renewed fervour, the goodness of the Lord and of His sweet mother is invoked, so that the sick may be healed. The Mother of Mercy is readily touched; she has pity for the sufferings of those who pray to her, and mediates healing to the sick on behalf of whom prayers are said. Thereupon the sick and the frail jump down from the carts, throw away their crutches, and hurry to the altar to thank their Benefactress. The blind, seeing and filled with joy, walk with confidence. Those with dropsy are freed from their swellings and at the same time from their harmful thirst.... Such are the night vigils, the divine vigils, the camps of the Lord, the new piety, the new divinely inspired custom. There is nothing of the flesh therein; one sees nothing earthly, only the heavenly.... This holy custom began in Chartres and was confirmed amongst our people by countless virtues. Thereafter it spread throughout almost the whole of Normandy, and took a firm hold in all places that were consecrated to the Mother of Mercy.[30]

Similar reports have also come down to us from others. A little later, the nobleman Guy de Bazoches wrote to his sister Aélide, Lady of Château-Porcien, about the building of the Church of Notre Dame at Châlons-sur-Marne:

At the building of this shrine to the Virgin, there occurred, to the honour of the holy Mother of God, a miracle accompanied by many signs, which no human power, no art, and no device could possibly have brought about. For which king, which potentate, except for Him alone,

Facing page
A view of the flying buttresses of the south nave of Chartres cathedral.

whose mere nod shakes the world, can straightway turn all hearts? One sees here how people of noble descent, of public power and high rank, renounce all worldly pomp and bend the neck of their hearts and bodies under the yoke of piety, while attesting to the words of Him who said: 'My burden is light'. The Holy Ghost, who mysteriously overshadowed the Virgin, kindles in His faithful such a strong love, that they are not satisfied merely to honour the church with generous alms, but, for the building of the mighty cathedral, themselves load the carts and wagons with heavy stones and immense boulders, and drag these to the site from far afield. Noblemen and noblewomen rush eagerly to seize the rope with which the heavy loads are pulled, and to place it on their shoulders, as if with this rope the land of promise itself were delivered unto them! And when the carts have been brought to the town, there too one sees noble-minded warriors, powerful matrons, youths and virgins, old men and boys barefooted rushing from all the streets and alleys in joyful competition. Many attach themselves to the rope, and those who do not succeed in doing so use their hands, linked to one another, for pulling. There are many to replace those who fall out from exhaustion. The ones help the others, each wants to share in the burden of the other, with the result that the brightness of virtue shines redoubled in all. Here the wolf goes along with the lamb, the panther with the kid and the calf, the lion with the sheep. And the one who drives them is but a tiny child, a new-born babe, newly descended from the angels into this world, and Who is of one essence with His Father. Yet others join those who are united in the pious work, and encourage them to virtue and consolation with drumming and singing, with zithers and cymbals, with wind instruments and holy, high-sounding choirs. With joyful dance, loud rejoicing, and great praise, they accompany the people to the venerable church of the noble Virgin, where, amidst psalm-singing clergy, the priest, who ministers to the divine helpers, sprinkles those exhausted by work and heat with the holy dew of consolation.[31]

The Royal Door

BETWEEN the years 1140 and 1150 the three-part doorway on the west front of Chartres cathedral was constructed. This has always been called the Royal Door, because the upright figures on the door-supports in part represent kings and queens of the Old Covenant.

The style of this door is still Romanesque in its reposeful equilibrium, and yet it is already Gothic in that the repose of its parts no longer strives earthwards, but upwards, as if these parts rose aloft like lights burning motionlessly. The forms are still austere and enclosed within themselves; they deliver themselves up as little to the uncertain light that changes constantly from morning to evening, as to the uncertain movements of the human soul. Bright and dark areas are created by smooth and rough surfaces (themselves fluted, jagged, or broken up by ornaments), with an effect rather like colours, and indeed, at one time they were actually coated with gold and other colours. The original coating has now gone, but a still extant enamel – a mild, melodic brightness encasing the rawness of the stone – covers the surfaces and articulations.

From the point of view of their deepest meanings, the images on the threefold Royal Door represent the most complete expression of doctrine that has ever been incorporated in the walls and supports of a doorway. Christ appears three times, each time in the middle of a tympanum: above the right-hand entrance, we see Him freshly descended to earth, sitting on the lap of His enthroned Mother; above the left-hand entrance, He ascends to Heaven, surrounded by angels; and on the central tympanum, He reveals Himself in His eternal majesty. The Nativity seems to indicate Christ's human nature, and the Ascension His Divine nature; but the immediate reference is simply to His coming and His going, to the fact that He is the alpha and omega of earthly existence, between which two extremes His eternal majesty stands, like the present moment between yesterday and tomorrow. These are the three different meanings of the Door – the Door that is Christ Himself.

Romanesque wall statue on the main door of Ferrara cathedral.

The lower portion of the whole doorway represents earth, and the upper portion Heaven. For the figures on the door pillars, though their names are unknown, are certainly representatives of the Old Covenant, and the earthly forefathers of the Divine Incarnation. Like the Incarnation, they bear the Heaven of the tympanums. Between these lower and upper domains, and interrupted only by the entrance doors themselves, runs the exquisite row of capitals, on which all the main incidents in the life of Christ are successively portrayed: it is like the demarcation line between two worlds.

That the figures on the door pillars seem so tall and narrow signifies that they themselves are the 'pillars of the Church', to which St. Paul refers in the Scripture. Durand de Mende writes: 'The pillars of the Church are the bishops and the learned divines who keep the Church upright. . .'. Strictly speaking, the door pillars and the figures associated with them represent a kind of ante-chamber, just as does the Old Covenant with regard to the New. In a similar doorway at Le Mans, this division into ante-chamber and main body of the church is overt: the forward wall pillars are all decorated with Old Testament personalities, while the

doorposts themselves are decorated with statues of the Apostles. The latter alone belong to the 'body' of the Church.

In the pictorial or sculptural decoration of a building, medieval art – especially Romanesque and early Gothic – bases itself on the meaning that inheres in each of its constituent parts as a result of its structural role. At the beginning, on the doors of some Romanesque churches, the spiritual meaning of the supporting pillars was indicated only by flat chiselled figures; one hesitated to bestow three dimensions on a human representation, and thus to detach it from the body of the building; a free-standing statue resembled too much the ancient idols. As, however, the figures carved on the door-posts or pillars began to take on from them their round or multi-facetted form, they became as if round figures themselves, and finally emerged from out of the building structure, without however detaching themselves from it completely. In this way the pillar, thanks to its spiritual meaning, gave birth to the statue, just as had also occurred in ancient times.

As a sign that the sculpted Old Testament patriarchs or prophets are incorporated in the eternal edifice of the Heavenly Jerusalem, one can see over their heads – not over all of them but over those on the right- and left-hand doors – a small building crowned with a tower.

The feet of the sculpted figures rest either on a calyx of petals (which gives them an astonishing similarity to the sacred statues of the Far East) or on monsters, seen as the vanquished might of the passions and of the devil.

The unusually large number of female figures amongst these Old Testament personages – eight have been preserved – points to the redemptive role of the Virgin Mary, the Protectress of the Church. She appears herself in the right-hand tympanum with the Divine Child, whose Nativity is represented there. On the lowest panel of the tympanum are depicted the Annunciation, the Visitation, the Nativity, the Adoration of the Shepherds, and, on the middle panel, the Presentation of Jesus in the Temple. In the Nativity scene, the Virgin rests on a bed that resembles a chest; a table covers this, like the sky or the heavens. On top of this table lies the Child in a basket, and an ox and an ass (of which only traces now remain) stretch out their heads towards Him. The table is not only the crib in which the newly-born Christ-child lies, but also the altar on which the body of the Saviour is forever sacrificed.[32] At the same time He is present on the other altar, portrayed immediately above, on which the mother offers her Child to the priest. The resting mother in the lowest panel, the temple altar in the middle panel, and the Virgin and Child in the uppermost panel (surmounted by a baldachin) are all situtated centrally; for it is the same mystery expressed three times over: the Blessed Virgin is the foundation, the altar, and the throne of the manifestation of God in human form. The way in which the artist has expressed the theological truths by the very geometry of the representation bears witness to his mastership: in the lowest panel, the horizontal, resting position of the mother, with the Child portrayed above her, represents passive resignation, by means of which the Virgin, affirming the will of God, becomes the 'substantial cause' of salvation. In her pure receptivity, open to grace, she is comparable to the *materia prima* of both the world and the soul. On the middle panel, the altar rises vertically, and on it the Child stands upright as His mother offers Him to the priest of God: she offers herself in the form of her Child, just as the soul must offer itself. In the figure of the Queen of Heaven in the topmost section, two concentric circles may be inscribed: the larger one surrounds the mother, the smaller one the Child on her lap, just as the nature of the mother surrounds on all sides the nature of the Child, and just as the soul

Facing page
Three figures from central portal of the west front of Chartres cathedral.

The tympanum, the Door of the Virgin, the west front of Chartres cathedral.

that has reached true knowledge contains in its centre the Divine Light, Emmanuel.

As the lowest and the highest in creation the Virgin appears in the manner described by Dante in the famous verses that he puts in the mouth of St. Bernard: *Vergine madre, figlia del tuo figlio, ùmile ed alta più che creatura* ('Virgin mother, daughter of thy son, lowly and exalted more than any creature').

St. Albert the Great wrote of the Virgin: 'Her son is King of Kings and Lord of Lords; so she must be called Queen of Queens and Lady of Ladies . . .. Her son is called God of Gods; so she must be called Goddess of Goddesses.'[33] This is the meaning expressed by the representation of Mary with her Child sitting on the throne, which, taken from a Byzantine model, has an even more peaceful and inaccessible aura because of the two angels swinging censers, who, like doves beginning their flight, rush to the centre represented by the figures. Their blazing deportment contrasts with that of the other two angels, on the tympanum of the left-hand door, who bear Christ aloft in a cloud and, in so doing, fall back overpowered by the Divine Light.

According to the medieval theologians the Virgin Mary, by virtue of the innate perfection of her soul, possessed in natural fashion all the wisdom of which man is capable. A direct reference to this wisdom is to be found in the allegories of the Seven Liberal Arts which, just outside an inner circle of adoring angels, decorate the tympanum of the Door of the Virgin. In the medieval context the seven sciences – which were classified as the *trivium* of grammar, dialectic and rhetoric and the *quadrivium* of arithmetic, music, geometry and astronomy – were not exclusively empirical sciences, as are those we know today. They were the expression of so many faculties of the soul, faculties demanding harmonious development. This is why they were also called arts.

Following an ancient tradition, Dante, in his *Convivio*, compares the Seven Liberal Arts to the seven planets, grammar corresponding to the Moon, dialectic to Mercury, rhetoric to Venus, arithmetic to the Sun, music to Mars, geometry to Jupiter, and astronomy to Saturn. The creators of the Royal Door of Chartres were certainly aware of this correspondence. It is thus doubly significant that on the tympanum of the left of the three doors the signs of the zodiac are displayed. These belong to the unchanging heaven of the fixed stars and thus represent the kingdom of the Divine Spirit, to whom this door, with its representation of the ascension of Christ, is dedicated. The seven planets, on the other hand, govern, according to the ancient viewpoint, the world of the soul. And Mary is the human soul in all its perfection.

By means of the signs of the zodiac – not all of which, incidentally, appear on the same door, *Pisces* and *Gemini* having had to be transposed, for want of room, to the Door of the Virgin – the arches surrounding the representation of Christ's ascension (on the left-hand door) can be seen to represent the firmament. Beside each of the twelve signs of the zodiac the corresponding month is represented pictorially in the form of its natural activity.

These natural activities – one for each month – are the terrestrial reflections of the twelve signs of the zodiac. From them one learns to what extent the course of human existence depends upon the heavens: in seedtime and harvest, in work and leisure; for the heavens, in their cycle, bring heat after cold, dry after wet, and thus keep life in being.

This is significant for medieval art: in two tympanums and in the arches surrounding them, the whole cosmos is represented, in its three great divisions: spiritual, psychic and corporeal. Medieval man always kept the profounder order of things in mind.

ℭ

The tympanum of the central door is wider and higher than those of the right- and left-hand doors and has only two zones, whereas the lateral doors have three. On the right-hand tympanum, the successive images of the human mother, of the sacrifical presentation in the temple, and of the heavenly queen are positioned one above the other; on the left-hand tympanum, where Christ ascends, a host of angels, like so many flashes of lightning from out of a storm-cloud, descend upon the disciples gathered below.

On the tympanum of the main door, the image of the eternal majesty of Christ, which has been portrayed on so many Romanesque church doors, finds its most harmonious representation. One can inscribe every geometrical figure into this tympanum; it will always be in consonance with the ordering of the five figures and with the wave of movements which go out from the central figure and return to it. Between the curve of the arch and the almond-shaped aureole surrounding Christ – these forms which separate and re-unite – a breath or spiration goes back and forth, giving the whole image its life.

Christ is surrounded by the four creatures described by Ezechiel and John: the lion, the ox, the eagle and the winged man. These are interpreted as the eternal prototypes of the four evangelists and their fantastical animal form symbolically extends beyond the purely human the anthropomorphic representation of God situated between them.

On the innermost of the three arches angels surround the majesty of Christ, and the twenty-four elders of the Apocalypse, who appear on the two outer arches, look up towards Him. On the lintel, the twelve apostles are present in groups of three, and to their right and left are two prophetic witnesses, perhaps Elias and Enoch, who are to come again at the end of time.

☾

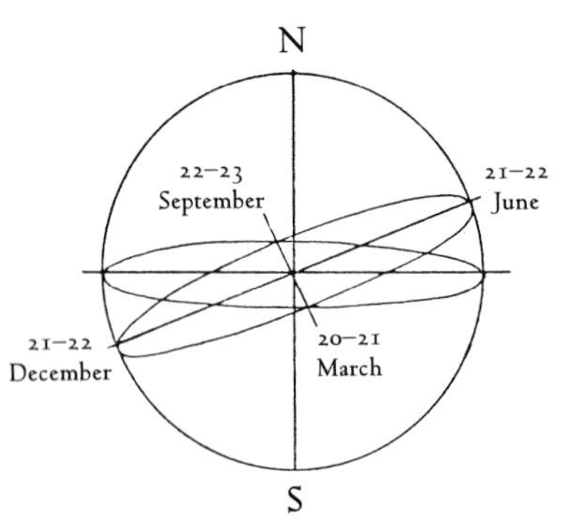

Scheme of the solstices

Why is the birth of Christ portrayed over the right-hand entrance, which lies south of the main axis of the church, and the ascension of Christ over the left-hand entrance, north of the main axis, given that north and south, according to their liturgical interpretation, correspond to the Old and New Covenants respectively? Presumably the physical positioning of the doors harbours an allusion to the ancient cosmic symbol of the *januae coeli*, the two doors of the heavens, known to the later Roman period.[34] Heaven has two doors, namely the two solstices; through the 'door of winter', the 'new sun' enters the world, and through the 'door of summer', the fullness of light leaves the world. According to an ancient view of things mentioned by Plato, the gods enter this world by the first door, and leave it through the second. The location of the winter solstice, which occurs during the Christmas season, is in the southern heavens, and the location of the summer solstice in the northern; it would seem that the representational order in the west door of Chartres cathedral is a direct reference to this: through the southern door the Divine Light descends into the world; through the northern it returns into the invisible. Between the two gates of Heaven stands the immutable axis of the world; to this the central door corresponds.

☾

We can now return to the Seven Liberal Arts. The order in which they are listed, when properly understood, testifies to a Pythagorean view of things, and this was not without influence on medieval art. The division of these sciences – and all their elements – into *trivium* and *quadrivium* came into Christian culture from Greek antiquity in a late and simplified form. The medieval spirit, however, was able to reanimate the integral vision originally inherent in it.

'Philosophy has two main instruments,' writes Thierry of Chartres, 'namely intellect (*intellectus*) and its expression. Intellect is illumined by the *quadrivium* (arithmetic, music, geometry and astronomy). Its expression is the concern of the *trivium* (grammar, dialectic and rhetoric.)'[35]

In fact the *trivium* was a schooling in both language and thought. It is language that makes man man; and that is why grammar comes at the beginning. Not without humour, the sculptor of the door of the Virgin has portrayed this art as a woman threatening with a rod two young children who are writing. The figures of the famous grammarians Donat and Priscian stand beside her. Dialectic, whose feminine representation in Chartres carries a scorpion and has Aristotle as a companion, is none other than logic. Rhetoric is the art of speaking, or rather, speaking in so far as it is an art; Cicero accompanies its allegorical figure.

THE SEVEN LIBERAL ARTS

Trivium 'the expression of intellect'	Grammar *language*	–	Moon
	Dialectic *logic*	–	Mercury
	Rhetoric *speech as an art*	–	Venus
Quadrivium 'intellect'	Arithmetic *number*	–	Sun
	Music *time (harmony)*	–	Mars
	Geometry *space (proportion)*	–	Jupiter
	Astronomy *motion (rhythm)*	–	Saturn

The four members of the *quadrivium* are likewise represented in a feminine form in Chartres. They are: arithmetic, with a reckoning board; music, with a glockenspiel; geometry, with a drawing-board; and astronomy, contemplating the heavens and accompanied by Boethius, Pythagoras, Euclid and Ptolemy. These four arts or sciences refer to the four conditions of corporeal existence: number, time, space and motion. Music, of course, is not only concerned with time, but also with sound; but it is in the realm of sound that time manifests itself most immediately and characteristically; otherwise we can grasp it only in movement, in which it is united with space.

'Everything proceeding from the profound nature of things,' writes Boethius, the great transmitter of the *quadrivium*, 'shows the influence of the law of number; for this is the highest prototype contained in the mind of the Founder. From this are derived the four elements, the succession of the seasons, the movement of the stars, and the course of the heavens.'[36]

It is a qualitative, and not quantitative, conception of number that lies at the basis of medieval arithmetic. It is thus less a method of reckoning than a way of understanding the nature of number, its properties, and the uniqueness of numerical series obtained by certain constant relationships.

That each individual number does not merely represent a sum of elements, but is in itself an expression of an essential unity, appears most clearly when one transposes each number into its corresponding geometrical form: three into an equilateral triangle, four into a square, five into a regular pentagon, etc. In each of these figures innumerable relationships occur, which variously exploit and demonstrate the law inherent in the figure concerned.

The connection between arithmetic, geometry and music can be seen from the fact that the relationship of musical notes to one another is rendered visible in the mutual relationship of the variously long strings which produce them. This can be easily demonstrated on a monochord, which has a single string and a movable bridge.

Following Greek tradition, Boethius distinguishes three kinds of proportions: the arithmetic, in which the same interval obtains between all members of the series, as, for example: 1,2,3,4,5,6 ...; the geometric, which progresses by means of a constant multiplication (a:c = c:b); and the harmonic, which unites the preceeding two, according to the formula a:c = a-b:b-c. The harmonic is the most perfect proportion: in music it appears as harmony, and in geometry as the 'golden section'.

The regular relationship of different movements to one another is rhythm. The day, the year, the lunar cycle, are the great rhythms which measure all change, and in this regard astronomy, the last member of the *quadrivium*, is the science of cosmic rhythms.

Number, proportion, harmony and rhythm are clear manifestations of unity in diversity, and also clear indications of the way of return from diversity to unity. According to Boethius, the essence of things is intimately connected with unity: the more unity a thing possesses in itself, the more profoundly it participates in being.

In medieval science, it is less a question of knowing many things than of having a 'whole' view of existence. Its method was anything but designed for the investigation of the material world and the furthering of technology. On the contrary: it possessed the means to open the spiritual eye to the beauty of mathematical proportions, and the spiritual ear to the music of the spheres.

☾

When today we say 'form', we mean only the visible and measurable aspects of a thing, especially its spatial contours. For the medieval masters, on the other hand – for the scholars and, in a certain sense, also for the artists – 'form' was the sum total of the essential properties or qualities of a thing; it was what constituted the inner unity of a manifested object. 'The forms of things,' writes Thierry of Chartres, 'are, outside and beyond matter, contained in the Divine Spirit. There, in its simple and immutable fullness, true forms exist. But those which, in a certain and not fully explicable way, are impregnated into matter, are so to speak ephemeral and not forms in the true sense. They are only something like the reflections or representations of true forms.'[37]

True form is thus neither limitable nor mutable; it is like a ray of the creative Spirit which, descending into matter, fleetingly lends it form. An analogy for this is artistic creation: just as the artist may more or less completely, depending on his humility, imprint on a material the spiritual picture that he carries within himself, so the essence of a thing may manifest itself more or less perfectly in that particular thing.

This way of looking at things is generally called Platonic, and so the men who taught in Chartres at the beginning of the twelfth century – such as Bernard, Gilbert de la Porée, William of Conques, and Thierry (who, at the very time that the Royal Door was being constructed, was chancellor of the cathedral School) – were all Platonists. Yet it would do them an injustice simply to attribute their thought to a philosophical school; in their works there is an element that transcends thinking as such, namely a genuine spiritual contemplation which, though far from being dependent upon words, nevertheless has to make use of words in order to communicate itself.

According to the Platonic point of view, all existence emanates hierarchically from the one Divine Source, which is neither diminished nor altered thereby. Can this perspective be reconciled with the creation story as related in the Bible? There is indeed a contradiction between envisaging a light which shines because it is in its nature to shine (and which one can conceive of in no other way than as shining), and envisaging a creative act which, at a given moment, calls into existence something that previously was not there. The masters of Chartres asked themselves this question and also answered it. When, with William of Conques,[38] one regards time itself as something created, the apparent contradiction disappears. Before the creation of the world, God was not in time: he was in Eternity, which lies beyond all time, in the eternal Now. One cannot say that God created the world at a given time, for time itself began with the world; from the standpoint of this world, existence (which shines or radiates forth from God) appears as if it began in time. In such a bridging of two apparently incompatible images, the more than merely mental character of spiritual contemplation can be seen.

The art of the Royal Door, in its inimitable and unsurpassed reconciliation of stellar farness and living nearness, is born of the same spirit.

Detail of head of Old Testament figure from central portal Chartres cathedral.

The First Gothic Cathedrals

ALMOST at the same time as Suger's re-building of Saint-Denis, the cathedral of Sens, the first cathedral in Gothic style, was built. Its main nave is still of squat proportions, less upward-striving than many a late-Romanesque minster, and originally, before the windows of the clerestory had been erected and the spaces between the vaulting filled in, it seemed even more solid. Nevertheless, the rib vaulting, and the way in which its sinews run together like a bundle of shafts and continue to the ground, is thoroughly Gothic. The logical coherence of the Gothic style of construction is already there, seemingly at one stroke.

Whence came the idea, and also the technical knowledge, without which no one would have been able to build these audacious arches? Certain elements are already present in Romanesque architecture, but the decisive model derives from far away, namely from Islamic art, with which the Franks had for long (since the beginning of the Christian reconquest of Spain) been in touch, and which now from many sides, at the time of the crusades, exerted an influence on the European world of forms. It is important to remember that from the year 1100 Jerusalem was the capital of a Frankish kingdom, and that the Order of Templars, which was founded in 1118 under the spiritual protection of St. Bernard of Clairvaux, raised on both sides of the Mediterranean its own army of building workers.

In Moorish Spain, in Córdoba and Toledo, there were cupolas supported on intersecting stone ribs. Closer to the Gothic style, however, are certain cupolas that are found in North Africa and, in their purest form, in Persia. They are characterized not only by being loosely set on a framework of ribs, but by spanning therein several surfaces or facets. In this way the ribs are scarcely visible on the inside of the cupola, but appear on the outside—usually a timber-clad roof—as pectinate ridges, which support the vaulting by their curved span. This unusual building technique, which differs from that of Gothic, arose because the cupolas, with their ribs, were built over a basket-like framework made of twigs. This could not be done in stone; in the case of stone, the ribs had first to be constructed for themselves, and only when they were entirely firm could the shells be placed on or between them. The ribs were thus transmuted from purely spanning to bearing elements.

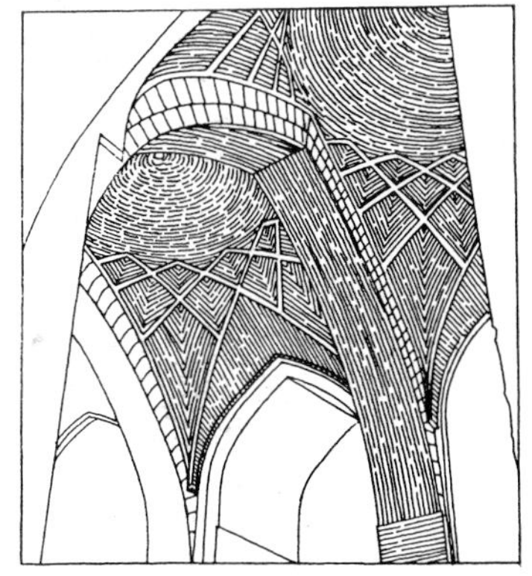

Brick vault in the Great Mosque at Isfahan.

That one should find the model for Gothic vaulting in medieval Persia is not surprising: French culture of the twelfth and thirteenth centuries readily adopted forms from the Islamic world, with which it was in touch, and especially those forms that were of Persian origin. This elective affinity is to be seen not least in the knightly epics of both sides. The generally Islamic influence, however, is prevalent in almost all the knightly forms of the medieval West; minnesingers and troubadours were stimulated by Arabo-Persian models, and the Christian knightly orders themselves would have been inconceivable without their Islamic predecessors, which based themselves on the Koranic precept for the Holy War.

What Gothic architecture has in common with its Islamic prototype is its joy in the geometrical play of lines, as well as its endeavour to overcome any impression of mass and weight. Both characteristics came increasingly to the fore as the Gothic style developed, right up to the geometrical web of late-Gothic vaulting. What is completely foreign to the Islamic prototype, however, is the way in which

Facing page
Pillars in the nave of Sens cathedral. Above the arcades, which open onto the aisles, runs the triforium, and above this is the clerestory, which originally was lower, so that the vaulting, in the manner of a dome, reached down to the windows.

the Gothic style incorporates the roof, stretched between the ribs of the vault, into the rest of the building. The 'braided' cupola of Islamic buildings seems to hover; it is only imperceptibly supported by the walls. Gothic vaulting, on the other hand, delivers its arches and ribs directly onto the pilasters and, through them, right down to the ground. This way of doing things was already present in French Romanesque architecture, in the clear articulation of the pilasters, directly linked to the ribs and the wall arcades of the cross vaulting. The architectural logic was already there and, in the Gothic style, the pillars corresponded exactly to the ribs of the vault as they converged downwards into a single bundle. It was because of this downward continuation of the ribs into the pillars that the walls became analogous to the shells between the ribs of the vaulting. Like these shells, the walls were little more than delicate partitions spanning the space between the pillars. The walls only assumed this character to the full when, thanks to the buttresses providing support from without, they finally became as it were translucent tapestries. Until that occurred, the interior of the cathedrals, throughout the whole of the early Gothic period, retained something of the weighty structure of Romanesque churches, even if the apparently elastic power of the arches, and the shafts rising to the vault in an unbroken stream and descending again to the ground as it were in a downpour, conferred on the whole building a hitherto unknown rhythm and tension, which, in place of the contemplative repose of Romanesque architecture, proclaimed a new upward flight of the will.

Articulation of the pillars in a West-Romanesque cross-vault.

A dome mounted on ribs from the Great Mosque at Córdoba and the interior of a late-Gothic tower-top from Strasbourg cathedral.

Romanesque architecture lets stone be stone; but it does enable its inert mass to be subordinated to a spiritual principle. Gothic architecture, on the other hand, introduces into stone an as it were upward-striving life and imperious will of its own.

This voluntaristic element in the Gothic style is connected with the fact that the predominantly monastic culture, which had given its stamp to the art of the eleventh century, had now been replaced by a knightly culture, which increasingly influenced life styles in the twelfth and thirteenth centuries, but which, having undergone excessive refinement at court, finally gave way to a purely city culture.

The knight is a man of will; for him, the whole value of existence lies in freedom of the will. But within the framework of medieval culture, this freedom had a completely different meaning than it had for the men of the Renaissance. *Vis-à-vis* his fellow men, medieval man was free through his dignity, which no one might impugn – and one must not forget that in the Middle Ages every social station or

View into the nave of Laon cathedral. The wall is divided into four sections, namely, arcades, galleries, triforium, and clerestory.

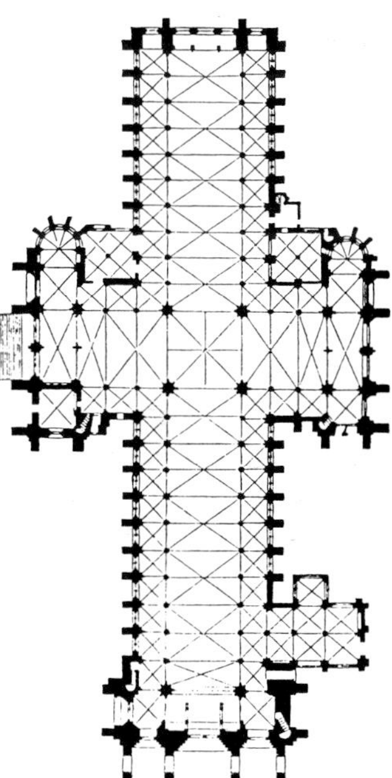

Groundplan of Laon cathedral. Each six-part vault over the nave corresponds to two bays in the aisle. The longitudinally quadripartite vaults of the transept are of later construction.

'caste', every trade or profession, possessed its own dignity and honour; such men were free in their own eyes, in that they were able firmly to follow a resolution once made; neither whim nor self-will, but fidelity to one's given word proves the inward freedom of man.

It has rightly been said that no other culture accorded such a high value to the pledged word. In fact, the social structure of the Middle Ages was completely based on concern for the inward freedom of the person, and this was so despite the distinction made between high and low, a distinction which, according to modern ideas, seems to disregard the freedom of the majority. Admittedly – and this is inevitable – outward freedom was unevenly distributed, whether because of difference in physical and moral heredity (on which, precisely, the natural order of social stations or 'castes' is founded), the presence of exceptional qualities, or merely property; but the hierarchy of rank remained just, as long as freedom and responsibility held the balance: the king or prince, who enjoyed the greatest freedom as regards authority over others, at the same time bore the greatest burden of responsibility, while the bondman or unfree peasant, despite his menial station, enjoyed the privilege of not having to worry about anything other than his own plot of land. He was tied to the soil, but he could not be driven from it; he was under the protection of his landlord, and as such, he could not be compelled to do military service.[39]

Even the king did not have the right, over the head of his vassal, to give orders to the vassal's men, for every relationship between lord and servant rested on reciprocity; the whole structure of the state consisted of a concatenation of alliances, which were maintained because they redounded to the advantage of both parties, but which fundamentally were guaranteed by loyalty alone, by the freely-given promise of the individual. What is important here is not whether this principle was followed everywhere and always; what constitutes the character of a culture is the universally recognized prototype. How highly loyalty was esteemed is directly proved by the outrage which any breach of loyalty provoked, and by the severity with which it was punished.

Characteristic was the rite of the oath of loyalty, by means of which the vassal pledged to his liege-lord the highest that he possessed, namely his free will, in return for the protection of his lord and authority over a certain domain: the vassal knelt down and placed his folded hands between the hands of his lord; the lord, to confirm the alliance, kissed the vassal on the mouth.

It was no mere coincidence that, at the time of the Gothic style, the practice of genuflection, with palms pressed together, was introduced into divine worship; an ancient Germanic custom and an essentially Christian conception here came together, for loyalty also puts an obligation on God; nothing puts an obligation on God more than the free gift of one's free will. Oaths of loyalty and vows both loomed large in the lives of medieval men. Sometimes these two forms of sacrificing one's own will coincided, as in the case of the symbolic investiture of the French king with the standard of St. Dionysius.

The factor of loyalty reconciles free will and hierarchical law. This is why the volitive element in Gothic art never assumes the titanesque or fantastical character which later, from the Renaissance onwards, became the characteristic of the creative will. In Gothic and, especially, early Gothic art, noble freedom and impersonal law are so closely wed, that it is impossible to separate them; and it is precisely from this that the liberating beauty of their forms derives.

Elevation of a bay and cross-section of Laon cathedral; also, cross-section of Noyon cathedral. The supporting pillars and buttresses do not belong to the original form of either church; they were added in the thirteenth century with the completion of the main vault.

The hierarchical law shows itself in the geometrical structure of the building: the cathedral of Sens was still built *ad quadratum*, as the Romanesque scheme, with its cross vaulting, was called. According to this scheme, every square bay in the nave has, corresponding to it, two similarly square bays, in each of the aisles. In their Gothic articulation, the vaults of the nave thus become six-part, for four of the ribs descend onto the supports of the main vault and two onto the middle pillars of the pair of vaults in each of the aisles.

The same quadratic arrangement, with six-part vaults in the nave, is also to be found in the cathedrals of Noyon, Senlis, and Laon, the building of which had begun about the middle of the twelfth century. It was first in Chartres that the cross vaults of the nave and the two aisles kept pace with a variety of breadths.

Without flying buttresses, which opposed the thrust of the vault from without, one could make the nave higher and slimmer only by means of support from the vaults of raised galleries at each side. In this case, the windows of the nave were limited to the uppermost of four stories, but light also streamed in through the raised galleries, which no longer looked like dark cavities, but rather, as in Hagia Sophia, like a translucent sheath. The cathedrals of Noyon, Senlis and Laon were built in this way. The cathedral of Notre Dame in Paris (with nave and two pairs of aisles), the first stone of which was laid in 1163, was, in its earliest and original form, also built according to the same principle.

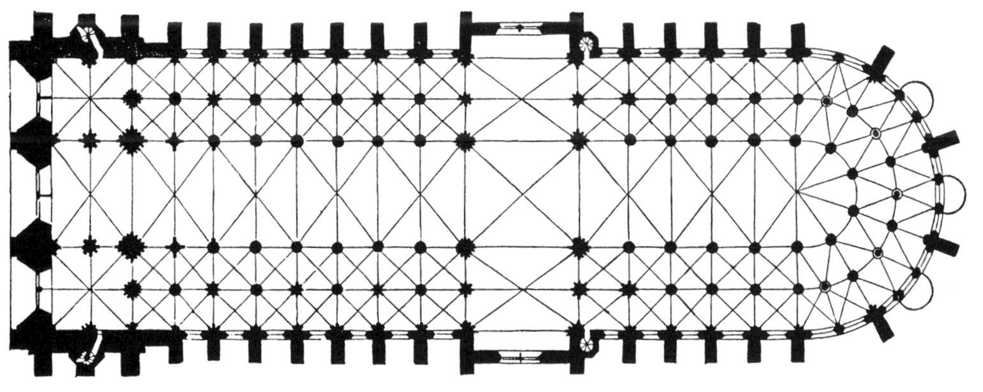

Groundplan of Notre Dame cathedral in Paris, in its original form, before the addition of the side chapels which today occupy the spaces between the individual flying buttresses.

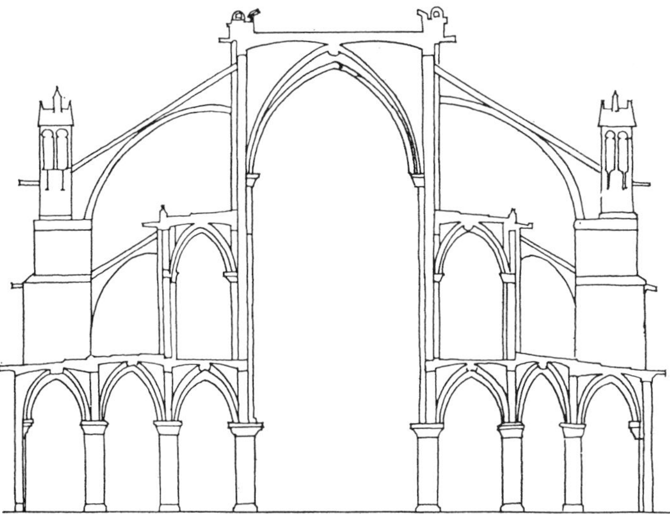

Cross-section and elevation of a bay of Notre Dame cathedral in Paris. Only the nave and the two pairs of aisles belong to the original form of the building (not the supporting pillars and arches).

Groundplan, inner wall and cross-section of Rheims cathedral. This is an example of mature Gothic construction, without raised galleries and with wide flying buttresses, which by themselves almost completely provide the illumination for the nave.

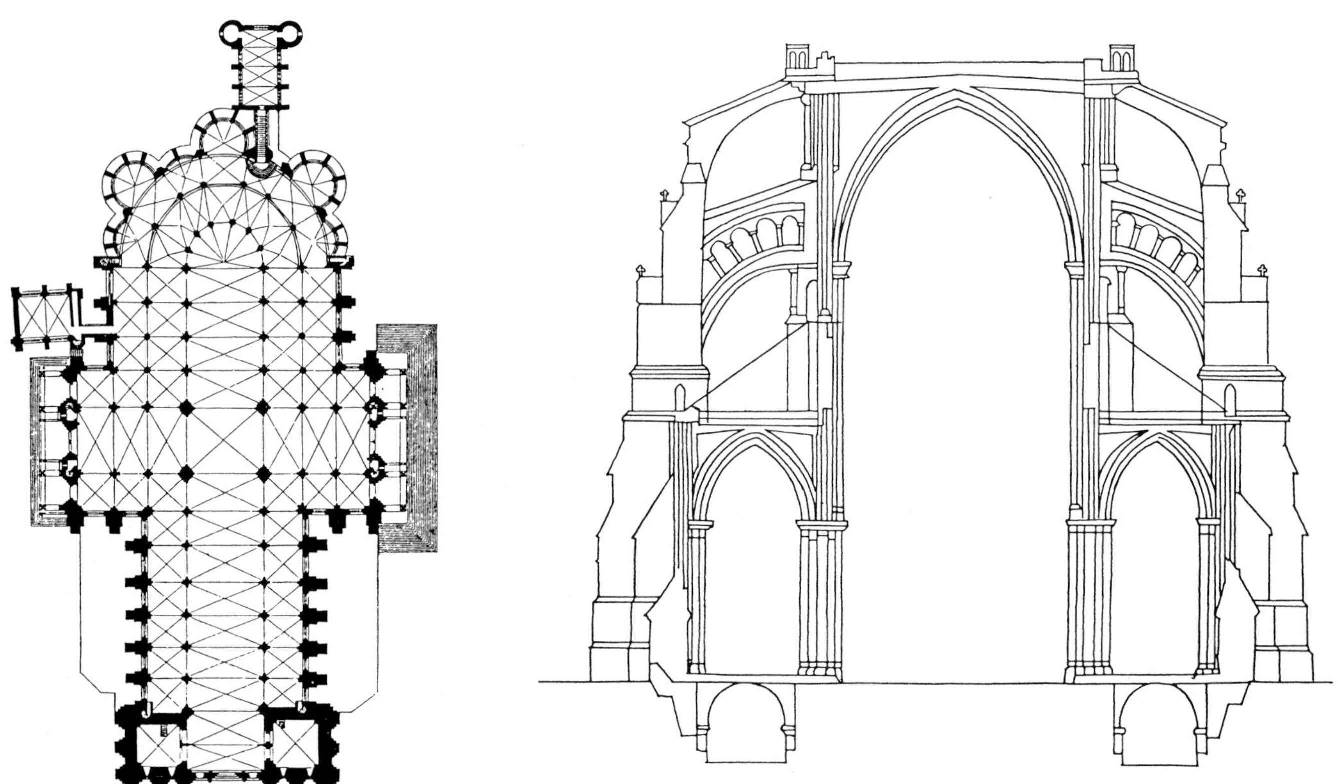

Cross-section and groundplan of Chartres cathedral, with its three-storey construction and its unique flying buttresses, adorned as it were with the spokes of a wheel. Underneath the aisles are the longitudinal crypts from the Romanesque phase of construction.

Cross-section and elevation of a bay of Beauvais cathedral, which represents a highpoint in Gothic pillar construction. Here even the blind zone of the triforium (the gallery under the saddle-roof of the aisles) is absent; the side walls of the nave, from below upwards, merge into a transparent grill of windows and arcades. The pressure of the vaulting is borne by a delicate forest of supporting pillars surrounding the nave.

The west front of Chartres cathedral. On the left, the northern tower, with the Romanesque base and Gothic spire; on the right, the southern tower, which was built in its entirety in the twelfth century. Before the fire of 1194, the façade between the two towers consisted of only two stories: the doorway, and the three windows surmounting it. (Above these windows one has to imagine the gable of the erstwhile nave.)

The Miracles of the Blessed Virgin at Chartres

TOWARDS the end of the twelfth century, the new west front of the cathedral of Chartres was almost completed: the Royal Door, which was originally intended for an antechamber situated behind the towers, was moved forwards soon after 1145, so that together with the towers, it constituted an unbroken façade, similar to those of other contemporary cathedrals. Above the door and between the two towers, the great three-part window was constructed; its profile was still Romanesque but, in its delicate width, it was already Gothic. The first three storeys of the north tower were built by 1145, and then the south tower was begun. (The bell chamber and crown of the north tower were added in the sixteenth century.) The south tower was completed to the top without interruption, and was one of the first typically Gothic church towers with a steeply rising and majestic spire. Soaring above the west front which was then only two storeys high, its effect was extraordinarily daring and powerful.

The three constituent doors of the Royal Door originally led into an antechamber, with a nave and two aisles, above which was a raised gallery.

If the new west front had been directly linked to the old building, it would not be there today for, on Friday the 10th of July 1194, the whole Romanesque basilica fell victim to a fire which overwhelmed the whole city. When the extensive wooden rafters of the church were in flames, the lead with which they were covered poured down in hot streams, so that no one dared approach where the fire was raging. The walls were split to their foundations, or simply fell down. Only the crypt and the new west front with its two towers remained undamaged.

The news of the destruction of the famous sanctuary spread terror and dismay throughout the land. A chronicler writes:

> The inhabitants of Chartres, both clergy and laity, whose houses and movable goods had been almost completely destroyed, mourned nothing so much as the destruction of their church, and reckoned the damage that they themselves had suffered as but little. By far the greatest catastrophe for them was that, in all their sinful need, they had lost the palace of the Blessed Virgin, the glory of the city, the mirror of the whole region, and the marvellous house of prayer. It happened that a certain cardinal and apostolic legate of the Roman church, named Melior, was present at the time, and saw the dreadful situation with his own eyes. This moved him so deeply that he summoned the bishop and the canons to a meeting; with divine words, he urged them to restore the lost glory, and called on them to do penance. Thereupon the bishop and the priests decided unanimously to devote a considerable portion of their income during the next three years to the restoration of the church.
>
> When the people of Chartres were unable, for a few days, to see the most holy relic of the Blessed Virgin, this was experienced by them as an incredible pain and sadness. The general view was that it was

pointless to wish to restore the destroyed city and cathedral, given that such a great treasure, the unique glory of the whole municipality, was lost forever. When, however, a few days later, the people, at the behest of the clergy, flocked to the place where the church had previously stood, and saw how the relic had been removed from the crypt and was now borne in procession by bishop and deacon, there arose so many voices of praise and jubilation, so many prayers of thanksgiving to God and His holy mother, that it defies description. Everyone was so overcome with joy that tears flowed freely and, throwing themselves on the ground, people prayed humbly and fervently to God, thanking Him that, in the midst of the conflagration, He had saved the incomparable relic for which the city was renowned. In fact, during the fire, the relic had been carried by a few priests into the lower crypt, the entrance to which, thanks to the foresight of our ancestors, lay close to the altar of the Blessed Virgin. Entrapped down below, these men did not dare to return through the flames that were now unleashed, but they were saved from death by the protection of the Blessed Virgin, as the iron door, which shut off the crypt from what lay above it, stood firm against the crashing of the burning timbers, and kept out both the molten lead flowing down from the roof and the enormous masses of burning cinders. When finally they returned safe and sound from the fury of the flames—having been presumed dead from the effects of smoke and heat—all present were overcome with joy, and hailed the priests with a jubilation mixed with tears, as if they had returned from death....

The people of Chartres reconciled themselves to the tragedy and decided incredibly quickly to restore the cathedral: it was understood from the start that a completely new building was required. Carts for the transport of stones were brought forth, and each man encouraged the next to get everything ready that might be necessary for the construction, or to have it prepared by craftsmen. Nevertheless, the gifts and offers of help of lay people would not have sufficed for the construction of such a building if the bishop and his canons had not, as mentioned above, agreed to donate a large part of their salaries during a period of three years. When, however, this three-year period came to an end, the financial means suddenly failed; those in charge of construction could no longer pay the workers their wages, and did not know how to obtain any further money. I remember that at the time someone said, moved by I know not what prophetic spirit, that the money bags would fail sooner than the money necessary for the building of the cathedral.... As human help was out of the question, divine help was near; for the Blessed Mother of God willed that a new and incomparable church be built in which she could manifest her miracles....[40]

The first of a whole series of miracles, which everyone interpreted as an invitation from the Blessed Virgin to re-build her 'palace', was the healing of a boy. A soldier, who had committed an act of unchastity with a servant girl in the porch of the church, cut out the tongue of a boy who had been a witness:

mutilated, he immediately began to praise God in a loud voice, as if his tongue were normal. All who knew him and heard him were astounded, and joyfully offered thanks a thousand-fold to the glorious Virgin. The crowd surged so powerfully towards the miraculously healed boy that, in order that he be not crushed, he was lifted onto a wooden platform close to the shrine of St. Lubin, near the box into which people used to place their offerings, piously and gratefully, for the restoration of the sanctuary of the Virgin.... The following Pentecost, the boy's tongue was restored.... This boy, object of a double miracle, still lives amongst us, and is a living witness to the goodness and power of the Mother of God.[41]

A document conserved in the cathedral since 1198 relates:

Through this knife which was placed on the altar of St. Lawrence in Chartres cathedral, Raoul the mayor of Menonville declares, in the presence of and with the agreement of his wife Alarie and his daughter Hugoline, that he gives over to the said cathedral his granary in Menonville with three quarters of an acre of land adjoining it. Husband, wife, and daughter have together brought this offering to the altar of St. Lawrence, and not to that of Our Lady, for on the day concerned it was not possible to approach Our Lady's altar because of the enormous crowd of people who had flocked to it in order to behold the miracles which God and the power of the Virgin's merits accomplished there....[42]

Of like manner is the following testimony:

At that time, when, by the benevolence of the Mother of God, countless people flocked to the cathedral of Chartres and brought their gifts, it happened that the inhabitants of a town in the region of Gâtines called *Caštrum Nantonis* (Château-Landon), men and women, nobles and commoners, inflamed with love, made their way there with a wagon heavily loaded with wheat. They had already entered the diocese of Chartres, when some of them suggested that they should attempt to reach Chartres the next day, while others considered this impossible because of the length and arduousness of the journey. In fact, some of the more prudent amongst them bought bread and other necessities, while others made no preparation for the morrow. The next day, very early, they harnessed themselves to their wagon, and pulled it all day long with much toil and sweat. Just before sunset, and as the day drew to a close, they reached, completely exhausted, a lonely place called Canturana. Thereupon those who had made provision of bread and other means of subsistence congratulated themselves on their foresight, while those who had not done so, and could now find no one from whom to buy anything, lamented. But if the ones profited from their worldly foresight, the goodness of God and of the Holy Virgin did not leave the others in the lurch. There were amongst them a few fortunate ones who had kept in sacks some bread which they had bought for five farthings; when they saw that some of the people were going hungry, they began to offer this bread for sale to the hungry at the same price as they had paid for it, which was a sign of greater compassion than if they had handed it out to the others for nothing. When the Son of the glorious Virgin saw the compassion of the vendors and was moved by the need of the hungry, He worked from Heaven above an unusual miracle

Overleaf left
The Royal Door, west front, Chartres cathedral.

Overleaf right
Central typanum of Royal Door.

among them. Just as once, in the desert, He satisfied five thousand with five loaves which He multiplied, so did He now, to the honour of His mother, condescend to multiply the bread in the sacks, so that there was sufficient in them to satisfy all those who hungered. When however the pious vendors, full of amazement, counted the remaining loaves and the money they had received, they confessed aloud that for the sales they had received forty farthings, and that of the loaves which they themselves had bought, not a single one was missing.[43]

The chronicle of the 'Miracles of the Blessed Virgin in Chartres' reports many such incidents, of which we will relate one more:

> At the same time as the priests of Chartres cathedral, following the disaster of the fire, sent a few representatives from amongst their number to various provinces and sought contributions from the faithful by displaying certain boxes and relics, it happened that an English student from London, returning from university in France, entered a church at the moment when one of these representatives from Chartres was speaking of the fearful fire and, by his lamentations, moved the congregation to tears, so that he might the more easily implore them for offerings. While everyone, moved by the extraordinary eloquence of the preacher, approached the relics which he displayed, and gave generously, the student was also animated by a desire to give, but his love for a certain woman prevented him from transforming his will into act. He had in fact nothing with him which he could donate, except a golden necklace, which meant so much to him that he had vowed neither to sell it nor exchange it, no matter how great the need, as he intended to make a gift of it to his friend. He was thus in a state of confusion, and pulled in opposite directions by virtue and sin. His sense of piety told him to donate the necklace to the Mother of God, and the example of the others, more than the words of the preacher, drove him in the same direction, whereas his passionate and impure love for the woman, and the thought that he would return to her empty-handed, pushed him in the other. He said to himself, amongst other things, that if he were to donate the necklace, the priest might not give it to Chartres cathedral, but that he might conceal it for some purpose, or secretly pass it on to someone else, so that his gift would help neither the cathedral nor himself. And yet it also was clear to him that if anyone should do something with simplicity and purity of intention, this intention would make the whole substance of the act lucid and sincere, and that the fruit of any pious action could not be diminished by the misdeed of another. Then he fell back to considering whether the woman would ever embrace him again if he gave away the necklace, or if perhaps, if he had nothing for her, she would reject him. Then he recalled that whoever, having put his hand to the plough, looks back, is not worthy of the Kingdom of God, and that consequently, whoever puts his hand to his purse in order to give alms and then out of avarice withdraws it, as he himself was now tempted to do, is likewise not destined for the Kingdom of God. Thus did reason and passion battle against each other in one and the same person, until he finally appointed himself judge in his own affair, and the principles of reason and goodwill overcame the irrational

promptings of passion, even according to the words of the Lord, that the Kingdom of Heaven will suffer violence, but that the violent will nevertheless be destroyed by it. This lent him such strength, that he pulled from the depths of his sack the necklace which he had intended for his friend—who herself was called Maria—and, with humility and tears, offered it to a greater Maria . . . .

After leaving the town of Soissons, where he had made this sacrifice, and was on his way to the coast with a view to setting sail for England, he reached a house and asked for a night's lodging. The householder, who had several beautiful daughters, did not want to take in the young and handsome student, for, as he said, he did not dare to introduce his daughters to such a guest. Nevertheless, he would permit him to spend one night on the straw in his barn. As the student had no other lodging, he was satisfied with this. When, in the evening, having satisfied his hunger with a modest meal, he lay alone on the floor and fell asleep from sadness and fatigue, it happened that, awakening about midnight, he saw a great brightness descend from Heaven and suddenly fill the whole barn with a powerful light. He saw three noble ladies, with radiant countenances and noble bearing, approach him. One of them, of higher stature, more beautiful countenance, and more noble bearing than the others, came up to him and began to speak to him freely and gently, so that all sadness departed from his heart. 'Fear not,' she said to the amazed man, 'I am Maria, your friend, the Mother and Daughter of Jesus Christ, whose love you preferred to that of the other Maria, and to whom you gave the golden necklace that you had intended for her; because of this, you have deserved to enjoy my love in eternity. Therefore I have decided to say to you, as to a very dear friend, that you must henceforth show yourself to me as a faithful and chaste lover and that, when you have returned to England, you must not fall back again into passion and impurity. On the contrary, in order to give yourself more freely to my love, you must avoid the company of shameless women, and seek as secret a place as possible, where you may lead a solitary life and always look forward to my return. There I shall visit you and console you, and henceforth nothing will loosen the bond of our love. And so that you may not think that this appearance has been an idle dream or a ghostly illusion, see here the pledge of your love, the golden necklace which you gave me yesterday in Soissons, hanging from my neck.'

Geometric Wisdom

THE VOLUNTARY help of the people represented only the lesser part of the work that was necessary for the construction of a cathedral such as Chartres. In order to complete the work in the incredibly short period of about forty years – it was begun in 1194 and the vaults were closed as early as 1220 – a whole army of skilled craftsmen (stonecutters, masons, carpenters, masters of the art of stained glass, and roofers), not to mention foremen, were necessary besides the volunteer draymen who brought raw stones from the quarry at Berchères, sand and lime for the mortar, and tree-trunks for the rafters; and there were also smiths and wagon builders ready to repair tools and wagons as necessary.

According to all that is known of the construction workers of the late Middle Ages, it can be assumed that those of the early thirteenth century were already members of guilds, which guarded their professional secrets and exercised a certain jurisdiction in professional affairs.

The work was awarded to the master builders and contractors by the bishop and the cathedral chapter. A member of the chapter paid the wages from the building fund, which was maintained by alms and bequests. A master builder directed the whole operation; following the general directives of his patrons, he drafted the plans, and created a model on the basis of these plans; if this was approved by the cathedral chapter, he would then work on the drawings for the individual parts of the building in his specially constructed hut on the building site. Under his supervision and according to his instructions, the stone cutters would prepare the blocks of stone before they were assembled and mortared by the masons. Special marks indicated the position and order of the prepared blocks, and chiselled signs named the craftsman who was responsible for this or that stone. No fundamental differentiation was made between stonemason and sculptor; even the seniormost master builder began as a mason's apprentice, cutting cube- or wedge-shaped stones to serve as corner- or keystones, and then, depending on experience and individual talent, would ascend the artistic ladder. As can be deduced from the sketchbooks of the Picardian architect Villard de Honnecourt, the master builder had to be versed not only in the art of stonecutter, mason, and carpenter, but also had to know something of geometry, statics, and mechanics. He was responsible for everything, from the erection of the wooden scaffolding and the operation of the pulleys to the execution of the statues and reliefs on the doorways. In order to guarantee such a many-sided technical and artistic formation, there must already have been, within the building guilds, a true corpus of knowledge (*scientia*), that was handed down from master to disciple.

The powerful body of the cathedral grew upwards rather like an anthill; it itself constituted the main scaffolding for its own further construction: walk-ways reached by spiral stairways, that ran alongside both eaves and inner storeys, and later helped in the maintenance of the completed building, facilitated the delivery of materials to where they were needed. Heavy stone blocks could be raised up either by cranes located in completed stories or by pulleys. As soon as the side walls of the nave were raised, they were bridged by the rafters for the roof. The scaffolding necessary for the building of the arches was attached to them. At the same time, the crossbeams acted against the lateral thrust of the vault.[44]

Facing page
Chartres: the nave and clerestory windows on the north viewed from triforium in the south transept.

When one remembers that the finely drawn plans and elevations, which were produced and presented by the master architect (some of them have been preserved to this day), had, with the technical means available, to be transformed into reality many times enlarged, one can easily see just how unsuitable a purely arithmetic conversion must have been: there could hardly have existed measures with such exact calibration as to permit the smallest fractions of a fathom or a foot to be measured and reliably converted into larger units. A surer way was to make a geometrical schema the basis of both plan and building, such as, for example, the network made of equal squares, that defines the plan of Romanesque and early Gothic churches, with their alternating supports. When one knows the size of a square (which, in this case, corresponded to a smaller arch-unit), one can mark out the whole network on the building site, and then mark the position of the foundations of the walls and the arcade pillars. The Romans used a similar method for the siting of their cities and fortresses, and the Hindus mark out in like manner the plan of their temples on the building site.[45]

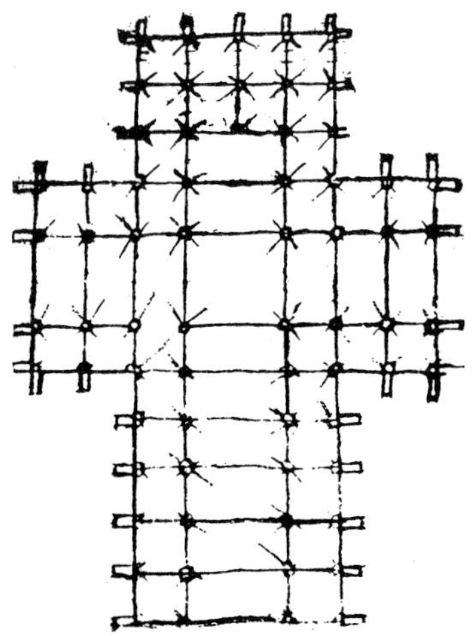

Plan of a Cistercian church, made up of rectangles; after Villard de Honnecourt.

More richly graduated is another schema, likewise derived from a square, by means of which the sizes of a building, from the largest to the smallest, can be expressed, not numerically, but in an as it were organic proportion. Villard de Honnecourt made this the basis of his plan for a bell-tower of Laon cathedral:[46] the various measurements for this are derived from a series of squares which are inscribed in each other diagonally; according to this, the relationship of the areas to each other is in the proportion of two to one, whereas the relationship of the sides of the squares is 'irrational', that is to say, inexpressible in simple numbers. The manuals of the stone-hewers of the late Gothic period say that right angles which have been derived from this proportion are sketched according to 'right measure'. Instead of inscribing a smaller square diagonally in a larger square, one can also inscribe the small square in a circle, and draw the larger square around the circle. Villard de Honnecourt provides an example of this in his design for the cloisters of a cathedral: the outer walls correspond to the larger square, while the courtyard or garden corresponds to the smaller square. Likewise other regular polygons may be inscribed within each other, so that their sides or diameters (of differing lengths) represent a continuously graduated proportion. As well as the square, medieval architects also used the pentagon, the hexagon, the octagon, and the decagon as basic determinants when committing the plans and elevations of their buildings to a fixed order of geometrical relationships. The square and the octagon were looked on as perfect forms, since they were symbols of a final condition no longer subject to change, the scriptural examplar of which is the Heavenly Jerusalem. The most perfect proportion, however, derives from the pentagon or decagon: from them is derived the 'harmonic' proportion, the 'golden section', which is characterized by the smaller element being related to the larger as the larger is to the sum of both (or inversely: the larger element being related to the smaller as the smaller is to the difference between the two), so that the proportion in every respect is endlessly uniform.

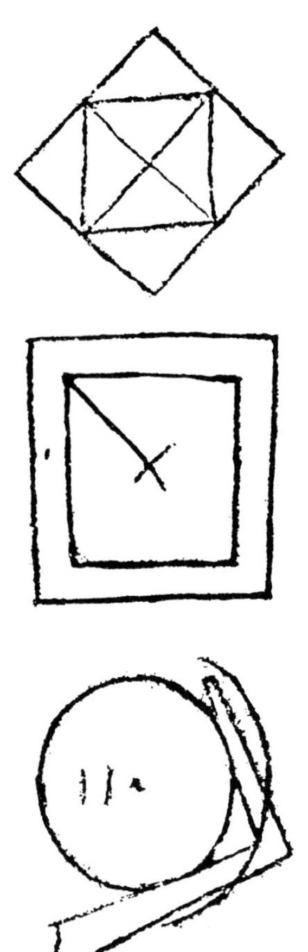

Examples of squares and circles related to one another in 'right measure', that is to say, as far as areas are concerned, in the proportion of one to two.

It can easily be understood what this application of basic geometrical forms means for the aesthetic effect of a building: by its means, all measures are related to a unity, and this can also be sensed by an observer unaware of the geometrical law lying behind it. This is so precisely because this unity cannot be expressed

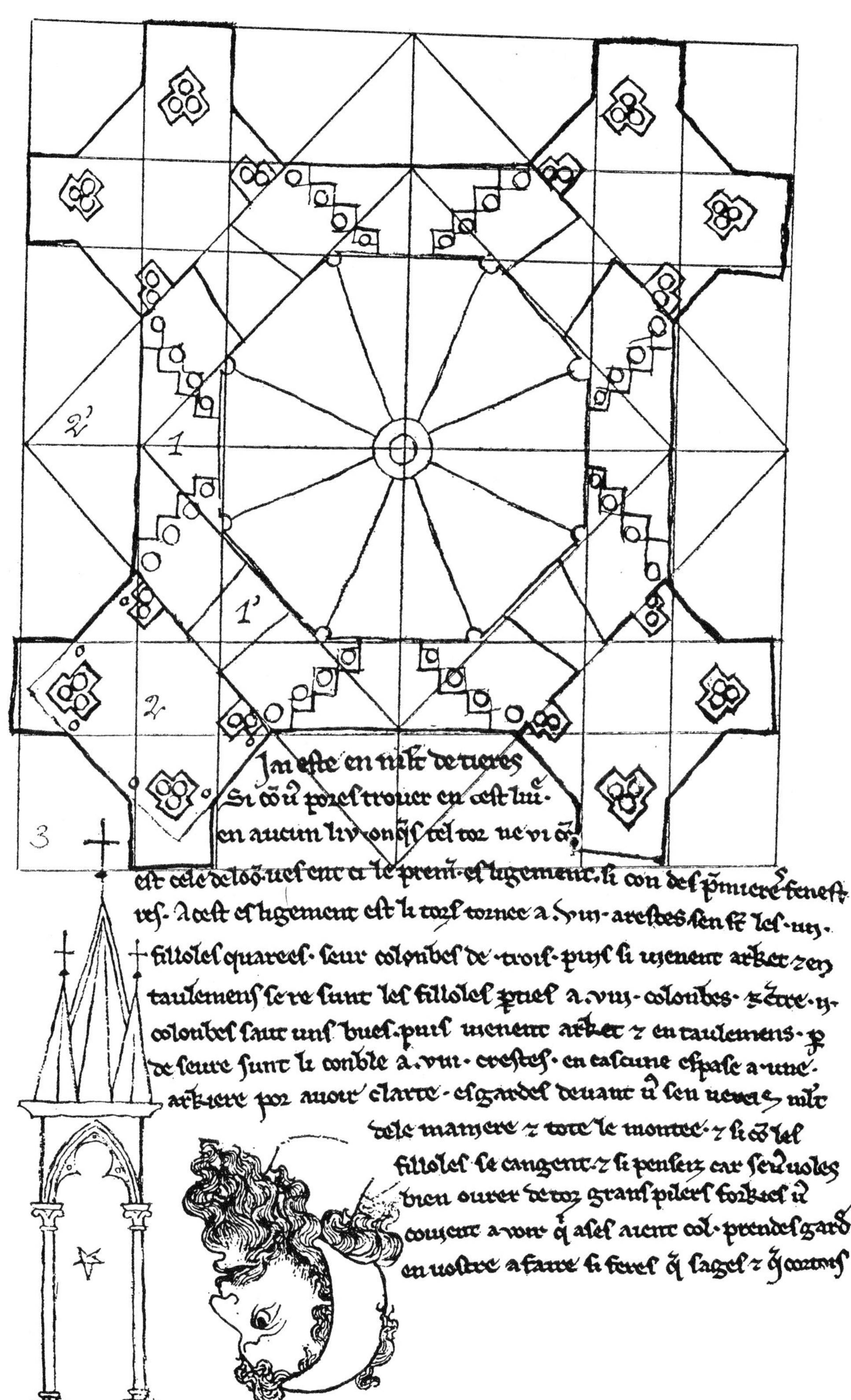

Groundplan of a tower of Laon cathedral; after Villard de Honnecourt. The geometrical grid, discovered by Walter Überwasser and outlined here, indicates the 'right measure' underlying the groundplan: it is developed from three squares inscribed one within the other, sometimes in parallel fashion, sometimes diagonally. The idea of placing the small towers at each corner emerges almost automatically from the basic figure which determines the proportions. It epitomizes the typically Gothic preference for limited spatial relationships, which are conceived more in geometrical-linear fashion than physically or plastically. *Nach rechtem Mass*, in *Jahrbuch der preussischen Kunstsammlungen*, Berlin, 1936.

quantitatively, but is a real or essential unity, and not one that is composed of parts. Nothing is as senseless as the opinion that compliance with a geometrical law might inhibit artistic creativity; were this so, one would have to regard the natural harmonies in music as inhibitory to the creation of melody.

In fact, there is a correspondence between geometric proportions and musical intervals. Indeed, the dependence on a specific set of proportions, derived from a regular polygon, finds its sonorous counterpart in the modal music of antiquity, the Middle Ages, and the present-day Orient: to each mode corresponds a particular scale, composed of two or three typical intervals and related to a keynote; and this confers a very specific 'mood' or quality on every melody deriving from it. Relying on the basic schema of the mode, the medieval musician could multiply his melodic patterns without ever 'losing the thread', just as the medieval architect, by remaining within the geometric order that he has chosen, could freely develop and change the individual elements of a building without any risk of losing the unity of the whole.

The use of a modal or geometric 'governing pattern' – which itself remains hidden, but which nevertheless harmoniously unites the various parts of a work – is in the last analysis the expression of a particular spiritual perspective, which Dante formulates as follows: *Le cose tutte e quante hann' ordine tra loro; e questo è forma che l'universo a Dio fa simigliante.* ('All things whatsoever observe a mutual order; and this is the form that maketh the universe like unto God.') *Paradiso*, I: 103–4.

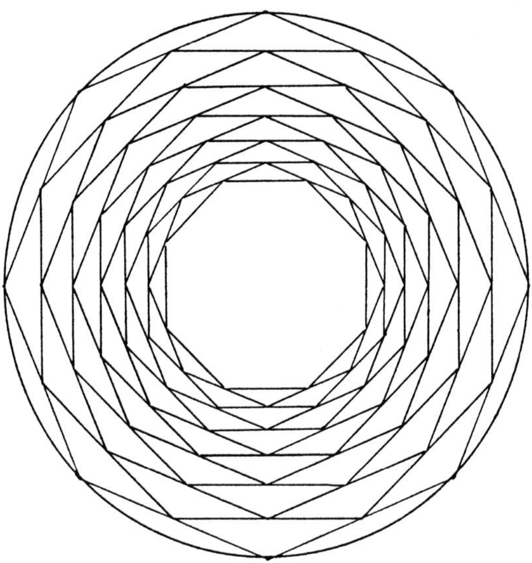

Rose composed of regular octagons inscribed one within the next.

Facing page
The west front of Laon Cathedral (completed around 1200), with its deeply set porches and its various component parts–rising upwards in a series of receding planes, and finally twisting and turning on the corners of the two main towers–has a much more imposing and dramatic effect than the west front of Chartres cathedral; as a result, it lacks the radiant peace that characterizes the latter.

It is not always easy to uncover the geometrical law governing a medieval building; for we do not know, from case to case, how the various sections were measured: whether from pillar centre to pillar centre, between the columns, from foot to capital, or from ground to springer. When, however, one can discern the geometrical schema, one is astounded to note with what sureness it has been applied. Although the cords under tension, which served to mark circles and straight lines, were subject to stretching, the measures are generally exact to within a few fingersbreadths.

It has recently been calculated,[47] that the south tower of Chartres (one of the few completely preserved bell-towers in a homogeneous early Gothic style) conforms, in all its measurements, to the proportional gradation derived from a rose of

octagons inscribed within each other. The regular octagon visible in the upper storey of the tower (which forms the base of the precipitously tapering crystal-like steeple) is thus the inner form governing all the rhythms of the building.

Another determining form, namely the pentagon and decagon, is fundamental to the Gothic reconstruction of the cathedral.[48] This is all the more surprising in that the anonymous master who planned the reconstruction, and probably also carried it out, had to erect his delicate Gothic space on the foundations of the Romanesque basilica of the eleventh century. This was presumably designed according to the quadratic scheme, even though its nave had no arch, but a flat roof of rafters. Apart from the foundations of the outer walls, which largely defined the outline of the whole building, there were also the crypts, which corresponded to the choir ambulatory and the aisles of the old basilica, and whose position determined that of the arcades of the nave.

The solution devised by the creator of the new building was to bring the separate chapels radiating out from the old choir ambulatory as far as possible into the overall space, so that they lined the eastern choir wall only as more or less strongly indented (and light-filled) apses. In this way a second and outer ambulatory was created, which continued on both sides into the aisles flanking the nave, and ran as far as the westernmost of the three 'aisles' of the new transept. The Romanesque basilica of the eleventh century did not have a transept. Only in the twelfth century were two small transepts (each with its entrance) added on both sides of the choir. The architect of the Gothic reconstruction situated his new transept much further to the west, in the optical centre of the whole building. It extends only slightly to the right and left of the nave, but represents in its great breadth (of three 'aisles') a kind of illumination within the forest of pillars. This already betokens the Gothic propensity towards a new and well-illumined concentration of space.

The intersection of nave and transept is broader than it is long, and the proportion of the two axes corresponds to that existing between the side of a pentagon and the radius of the circle circumscribing it. This intersection is an example of the geometrical law from which the proportions of both the plan and the elevations are derived.

The aisles, in keeping with the Romanesque arrangement, are half as wide as the nave, and this simple ratio of one to two joins with the harmonic proportion underlying the intersection to produce a perfect network of larger and smaller arches.

In contrast with the earlier cathedrals, the master of Chartres did not allow the nave arches to be greater than any of the pairs of aisle arches, but kept in step with the aisles, by dividing up the nave with short, but broad, arches.

When building Chartres, he followed the example of the cathedral at Sens, in that he left out the raised galleries, and separated the clerestory from the arcades only by the length of the triforium. For this reason, he let the clerestory rise higher (higher than any other master architect had ever dared to do), by directing the pressure from the vaulting, through the wheel-like flying buttresses, onto the pillars, which stand round the building like slim towers. Only by so doing did it become possible almost completely to fill the outer walls of the nave and or aisles with windows, with the exception of the blind zone of the triforium, corresponding to the lean-to roof of the aisles, which only later, in the cathedrals of Beauvais and Cologne, were also opened to the light.

Inside the cathedral, the nave is clearly and flexibly articulated, lengthwise

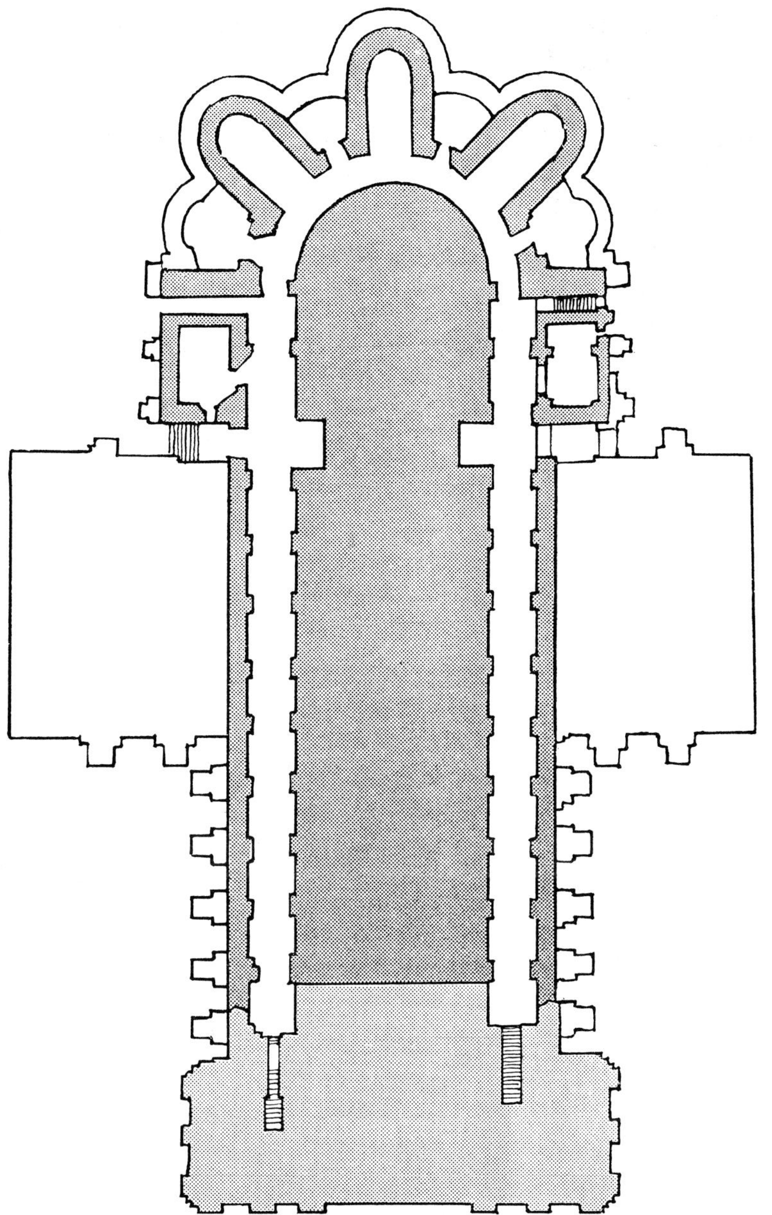

The foundation walls of Chartres cathedral at the level of the crypts. The foundations of the Romanesque basilica of the eleventh century are shaded darkly, those of the west façade are shaded lightly, and those of the Gothic cathedral are only outlined. See also the groundplan on page 99.

by clustered pillars, and vertically by simple horizontal cornices. The regular sequence of the pillars is transformed into a rhythm, in that round pillars surrounded by octagonal supports alternate with octagonal pillars surrounded by round supports. The gradation of the storeys is regular but not monotonous, because it is in keeping with the harmony inherent in the regular decagon, into which the pentagon (governing the groundplan of the building) is inscribed. The length of the intersection (of nave and transept) is equivalent to the height of the wall pillars (from the columns of the arcades to the start of the vault), and this is the same as the width of the nave (if measured, not from pillar-centre to pillar-centre, but between the columns) and the height of the vault in the aisles. If one starts from the total height of the nave (from the ground to the crown of the vault), the next smaller stretch of the 'golden section' is the height of the nave up to the beginning of the vault, then the above-mentioned height of the wall pillars (from the columns of the arcades to the beginning of the vault), then the height of the columns of the arcades themselves (from the plinth to the springing-stone of the arch), and finally the distance between the springing-stone and the lower cornice.

To this harmonic cadence is linked, as in the groundplan, the simple proportion of two to one, emphasized by the upper cornice on the wall pillar.[49]

The gradation of proportions just mentioned can be seen in the measurements of these individual parts; according to Otto von Simson, they constitute the following series: 36.40 : 22.46 : 13.85 : 8.61 : 5.35 metres. By means of geometry, however, still more harmonic relationships can be expressed.

For this is a clarity, a pure accord, which the observer 'sees' or 'hears' rather than reckons. And this explains why people in the seventeenth and eighteenth centuries, who used the term 'Gothic' to mean 'barbaric', liked to cover over the all too widely-spread rhythm of the stone body with neo-classical stucco statues, which they were able to 'understand literally'. But who could tame the upsurge of these arches, which starts already in the wall-pillars, and even in the clustered columns of the arcades? The arches are not merely laid on the pillars, nor are the pillars merely placed in front of the walls. All these things – arches, walls, and pillars – constitute an organic whole, comparable to the calyx of a flower, with its sepals and petals. The lily-like miracle of the high Gothic style can already be seen in the steeply rising divisions of the vaulting, even if in Chartres the basic stone, with its edges and curves, still remains rough; its heaviness is overcome; and wherever the vault-coverings join with the arched ribs, the steeply rising girders, and the stilted arcaded arches, they resemble leaves that have grown a natural growth.

See illustration on page 90.

The vaulting of a classical Gothic cathedral, with a three-story nave and quadripartite vaulting; after John Fitchen.

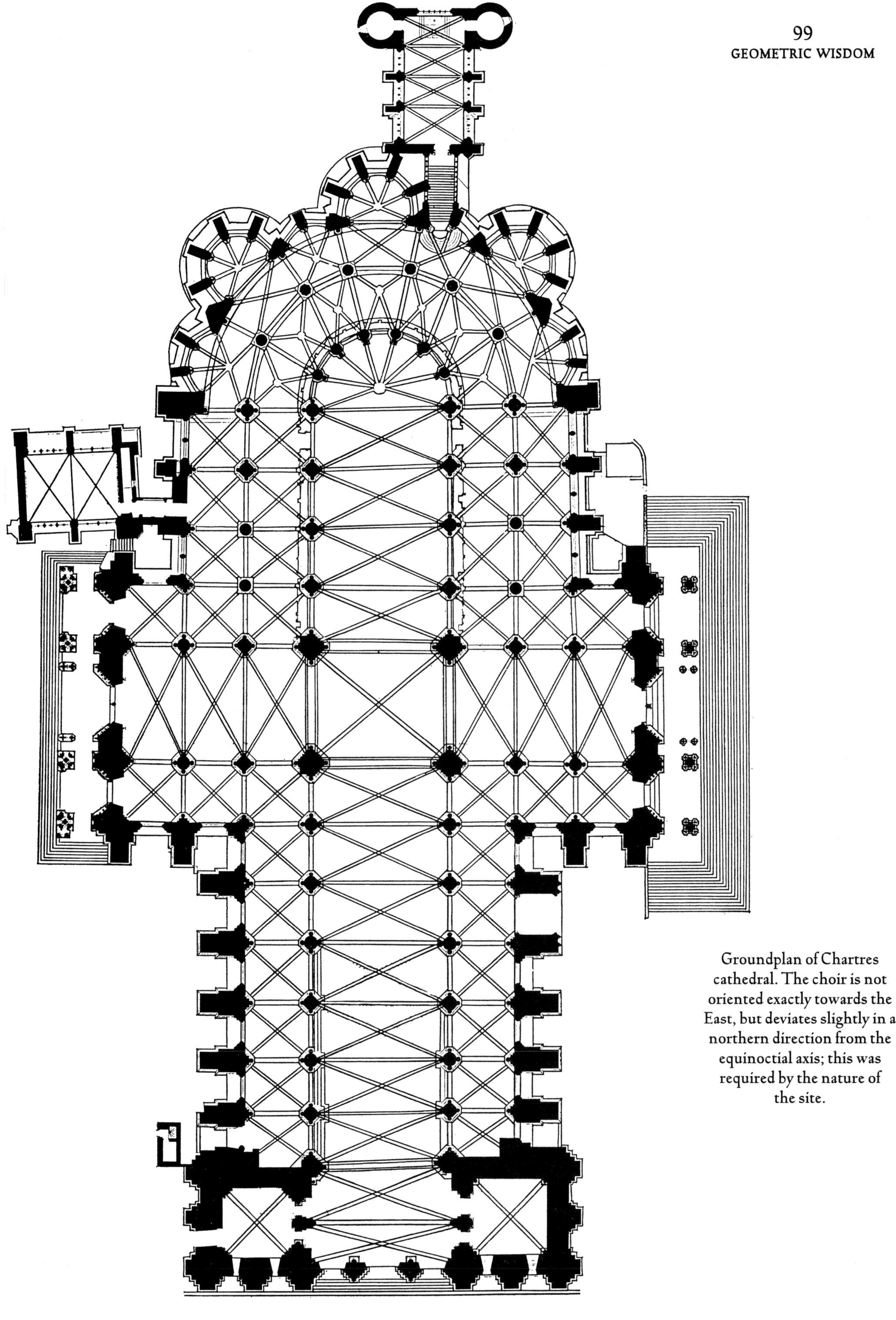

Groundplan of Chartres cathedral. The choir is not oriented exactly towards the East, but deviates slightly in a northern direction from the equinoctial axis; this was required by the nature of the site.

Section through the transept of Chartres cathedral, looking towards the choir. The late-Gothic partition separating the inner choir from the surrounding areas was not part of the original plan, which was chiefly concerned with the illumination of the inside of the building. From an engraving by J. B. A. Lassus.

Scotus Eriugena[50] taught that, at the end of time, the lower states of existence would be absorbed into the higher: the mineral into the vegetable, the vegetable into the animal, the animal into the psychic, and the psychic into the spiritual – not by any mixing of forms, but by the absorbing of the more gross state by the more subtle state. The form of the Gothic sanctuary seems to prefigure this upward transmutation.

☾

> As if to the limbs of a mighty body, God, by distinguishing between place and name, conferred on every nature its appropriate measure and its predestined role. In God nothing was confused; in God, before the creation of time, nothing lacked its form; for as soon as the stuff of things was created, it immediately took the forms of the species corresponding to it.... It encompassed everything. It strengthened the interior, protected the exterior, preserved the superior, and supported the inferior; it linked the various elements with unfathomable art, and united and reconciled opposites by a marvellous equilibrium, stabilizing the volatile, that it might not disappear, and supporting the heavy, that it might not collapse....

These words, written in the middle of the twelfth century (in connection with the history of creation) by the Abbot Arnold, who lived at Bonneval near Chartres,[51] enable us to see how, for the people of the Middle Ages, the building of a cathedral, even down to its most technical aspects, could be the symbol of creation.

According to the Bible, God created all things 'according to measure, number and weight'. The medieval thinkers concluded from this that measure, number and weight were so many aspects of one and the same order, and they found this confirmed in the laws of statics. According to the law of levers, for example, weights which maintain the balance when on different sides of a fulcrum must stand in inverse proportion to the length of the arms of the lever. Extension, quantity, and weight are thus mutually ordered by the law of proportion.

At the beginning of the thirteenth century, it was taught that the equilibrium of a body depended on the reciprocal cancellation of opposing forces;[52] this knowledge seems to be reflected in the construction of the Gothic cathedrals, and especially in the use of supporting pillars and flying buttresses. What emerges clearly is that the Gothic architects demanded geometrical unity in a building not only for reasons of beauty but also in the interests of stability. The architect Jean Mignot, who uttered the famous words *ars sine scientia nihil* ('art without science is nothing') to the builders of the cathedral of Milan, warned the Italians not to depart from the proportions that derived from the chosen geometrical schema; otherwise, he said, the building would fall. The Italians, to whom Gothic construction remained essentially foreign, replied that any element in an upright position could not fall down; nevertheless, to be on the safe side (and wishing to contradict Mignot's theory), they incorporated iron rods into their pillars....[53]

The determining geometrical figure, into which the front or side elevations of a cathedral could be inscribed (and which, for its part, could be inscribed in a circle), thus determined the equilibrium of the whole building, which lies, not in the inertia of sheer mass, but in the equilibrium of opposing forces. In fact, the cross section of a cathedral such as Chartres seems to be inscribed (along with the flying buttresses on both sides) in a circle which has its centre at half the height of the nave.

The whole form of the Gothic cathedral proceeds from the harmonically divided circle. As if to impress this principle even on the ignorant, there are the large geometrical rose windows that occupy a central position in the walls of the church.

In his *Convivio*, Dante says of geometry that it exists between two immeasurable greatnesses: the point, which is the origin of all figures, but which itself has no extension, and the circle (or the sphere), the form of which cannot be exhausted by division. Both the point and the circle are symbols of Divine Unity.

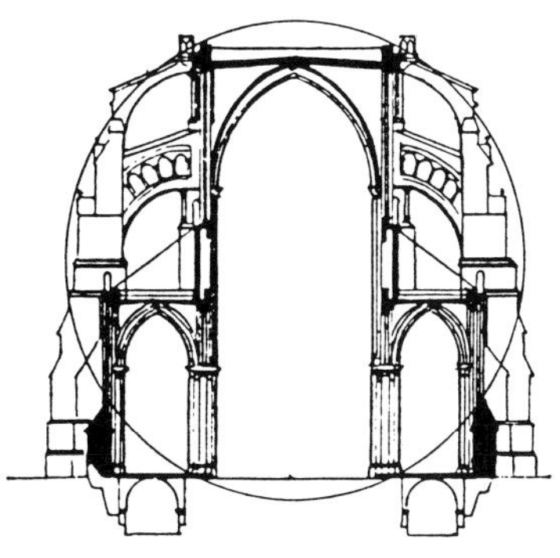

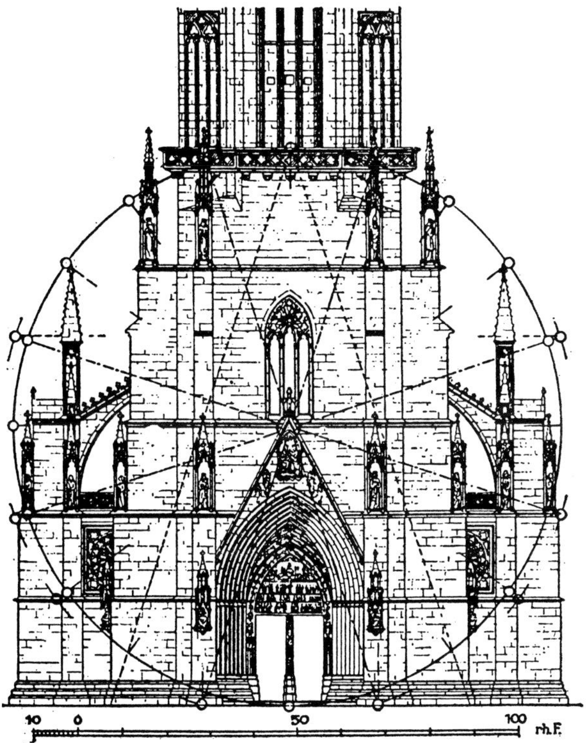

According to Rudolf Mössel, the façade of the cathedral of Freiburg-im-Breisgau is inscribed in a circle divided into ten.

Dante lived a hundred years later than the builders of the first Gothic cathedrals; his great poem, however, is their exact counterpart. He captured in words what one may call the Gothic *Weltanschauung*. If the great Gothic cathedrals had arisen in Italy, there would perhaps have been no *Divine Comedy*: spiritual *summas* in different arts never occur side by side.

At the end of his *Divine Comedy*, Dante uses a metaphor which confers on the dividing of the circle – the Alpha and Omega of the Gothic geometry of building – its profoundest meaning. In the Divine Essence, which appears to the poet as a three-fold circle of light, the prototype of man can be discerned:

Qual è'l geometra che tutto s'affige
per misurar lo cerchio, e non ritrova,
pensando, quel principio ond' egli indige:

tale era io quella vista nova:
veder voleva, come si convenne
l'imago al cerchio, e come vi s'indova.

> As the geometer who all sets himself to measure the circle and findeth not, think as he may, the principle he lacketh; such was I at this new seen spectacle; I would perceive how the image consorteth with the circle, and how it is inscribed within it. (*Paradiso*, XXXIII, 133–38)*

To know how to divide the circle in order to derive from it a particular figure, or, inversely, to know how to reduce a particular figure, through knowledge of its essential form, to the unity of a circle: this, for the medieval builders, was the quintessence of art. And because these procedures were incapable of schematic solution, but had to be modified from case to case, with appropriate insight and on the basis of a creative inspiration, it followed that to have acquired such an art was proof of professional mastership. Artistic sensibility and inward knowledge here came together, for the finding of the centre towards which all forms are ordered, is an outward symbol for the inward realization of the spiritual centre, the timeless centre in the heart, on which our very existence depends. Something of this can be detected in the customs and sayings of the late-Gothic stonemasons:[54]

> A point that goes into the circle,
> Inscribed in the square and the triangle;
> If you find this point, you possess it,
> And are freed from care and danger;
> Herein you have the whole of art,
> If you do not understand this, all is in vain.
>
> The art and science of the circle
> Which, without God, no one possesses.

* 'The problem loosely described as "squaring the circle" is stated by Dante with his usual accuracy. The radius and circumference of a circle being incommensurable, it is impossible to express the circumference exactly in terms of the radius – as impossible as it is to express deity in terms of humanity. The radius being the unit, then, the circle cannot be exactly measured. There is no difficulty in construcing (by means of a cycloid) a square equal in area to a given circle.' Notes to the Temple Classics edition of *The Divine Comedy*, Dent, London, 1899.

The Sacred Windows

THE INTERIOR of Romanesque churches was usually decorated with wall pictures; the walls under the windows, the semicircle of the apse, and often the flat wooden roof, offered themselves for pictorial representations like blank pages in a book. In the Gothic cathedrals, however, there was scarcely an empty wall for paintings; it is true that the capitals, cornices and ribs were overlaid with colour, and the inside of the vaulting was strewn with golden stars; but pictorial art was almost entirely confined to the tapestries of light that were the windows, which themselves increasingly took the place of walls. It is characteristic of Gothic architecture that pictorial decoration is not merely added to the building: paintings are not merely added to the wall, or attached to it like costly ornaments in relief; just as the statues hewn out of stone become like members of the building itself, in the form of pillars, ribs of arches and sills, so also the stained-glass windows belong integrally to the building, which, without them, could not be: the walls of Gothic cathedrals are not transpierced so that people can see out; they are intended as walls of light, or of luminous precious stones, like the walls of the Heavenly Jerusalem.

Pictures as walls, and walls as light: the light, indeed, only becomes visible because of the stained-glass windows. For in itself light cannot be seen; one can only see the objects that it illumines, or the blinding sun itself. By passing through stained glass, the light uncovers its inner richness of colours, and itself becomes an object of vision.

It is therefore no sophism when medieval symbolists compare stained-glass windows with the Holy Scriptures or with their human vehicles.[55] The transparent pictures are like symbols of Holy Scripture, through which the Divine Light is made accessible to human vision; in itself, in its unattenuated brightness, it would blind the eyes.

The refraction of the uncoloured light into a spectrum of colours is the most direct symbol of the fact that, in the Divine Being (the Logos, which itself is undivided), the essential forms of all things are contained. For colours are properties of light, and properties are essential characteristics, and thus are 'forms' in the sense that this word had for medieval thinkers.

Ulrich Engelberti of Strasbourg, a pupil of St. Albert the Great, and a representative of the intellectual perspective of the School of Chartres, wrote of beauty as follows:

> The essential cause of things resembles physical light which, though one by nature, comprises the beauty of all colours. The more the colours possess light, the more they are beautiful (the diversity of these colours is occasioned by the diversity of the surfaces that receive the light), and the more they lack light, the more they are hideous and formless; even so the Divine Light, which by nature is one, contains in itself, in simple and undifferentiated mode, everything that appears as beauty in created forms (the diversity of which forms depends on the diversity of the 'surfaces' receiving the Light); created forms are more or less unformed, the more or less they are unlike the primal intellectual light.

Overleaf left
The 'Christmas window' of the west façade of Chartres cathedral, with the Madonna and Child in a mandorla at the top. It comes mainly from the twelfth century, before the Gothic re-building of the cathedral. The windows of these early times are distinguished by the unsurpassable luminosity of the blue glass. The scenes are a pure mosaic of colours, in which only the essential features of the figures are portrayed.

Overleaf right
The central part of the west rose window. The scenes represent the Last Judgement. In the middle of the 'wheel' is the enthroned Christ, Judge of the world. He shows his wounds, from which the blood of grace flows. Groups of resurrected souls approach him, either guided by angels, or being turned away. At the top of the innermost circle, 'Abraham's bosom'—the place of the blessed—is portrayed between two cherubim. Below left, one sees the abyss of hell. This window is from the thirteenth century.

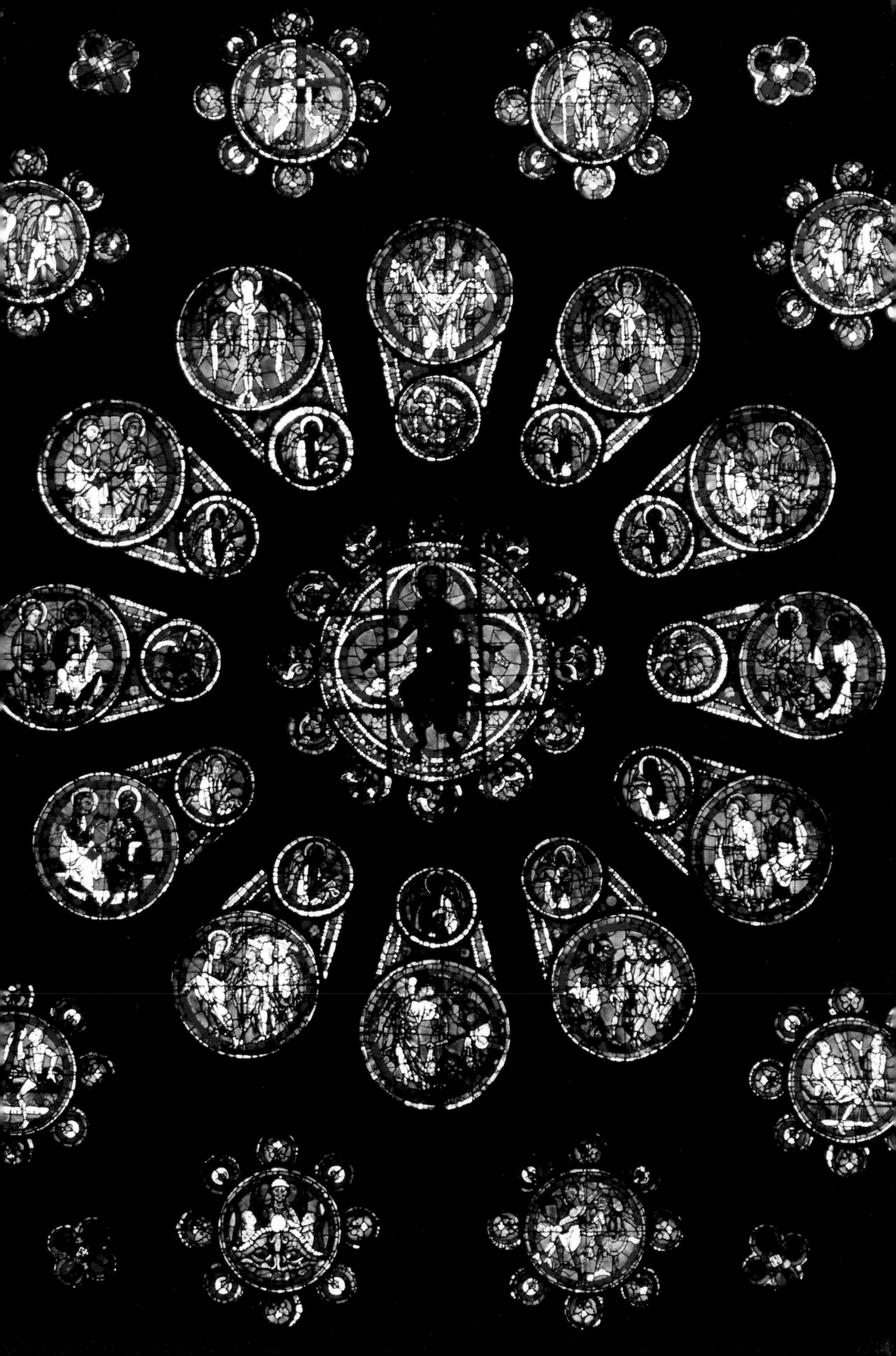

Therefore the beauty of forms lies not in their multiplicity; rather it has its cause in the intellectual light, which is one. For this all-containing Light illumines directly, and the more of this Light a form contains within itself, the more beautiful it is, and the more it resembles its Cause.[56]

Concerning the refraction of the Logos, from one level of creation to another, Dante writes:

> All that dies, and all that cannot die,
> is but the reflection of that Idea
> which Our Lord begat in love.
>
> For the living Light that so shines
> from its source, that it never separates from it
> nor from the love that dwells in both,
>
> Unites, out of goodness, its rays,
> as if reflected, to other substances, and yet
> the light itself remains eternally one and undivided.
>
> Thus it descends unto the lowest potencies,
> from act to act, until finally
> it leaves only the merest traces of itself.

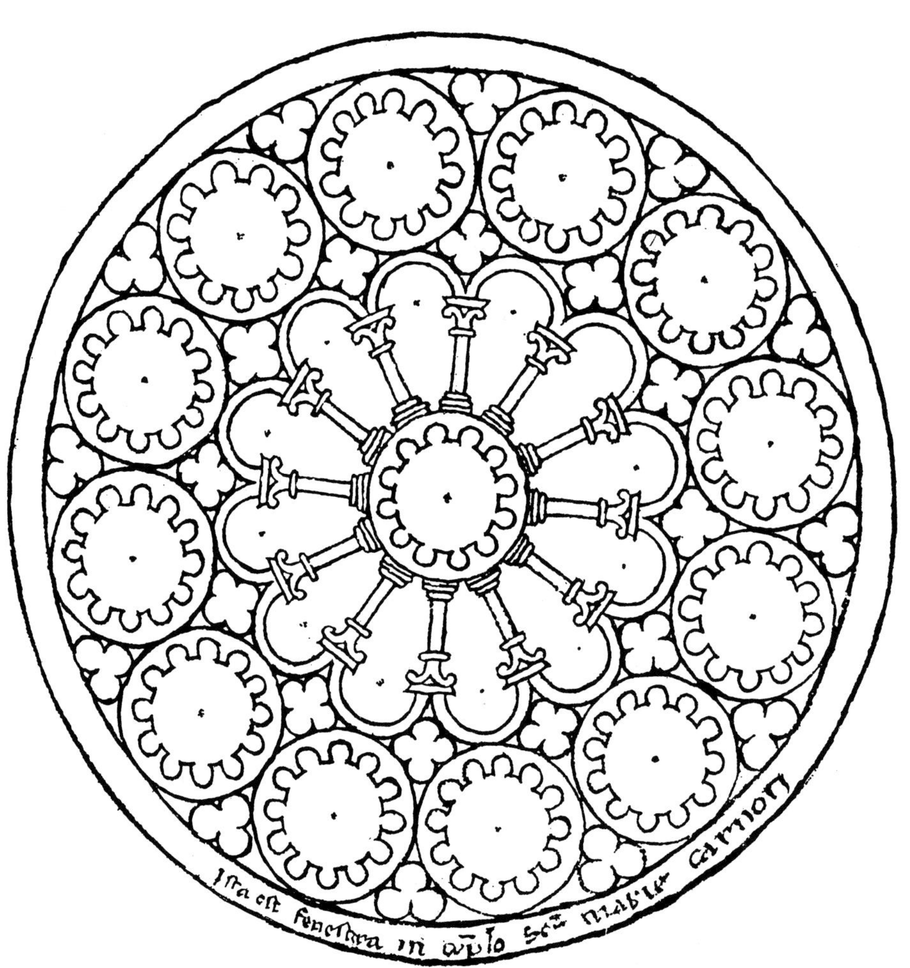

The wheel-window on the west front of Chartres cathedral, as drawn by Villard de Honnecourt in the thirteenth century.

By merest traces, I mean created things,
which, with seed or without seed,
the moving heaven produces.

Their substance, and that which gives it form,
is not of one kind, and so the Prototype
appears more in one and less in the other. *Paradiso*, XIII, 52–69

In the Orient and Byzantium, as also in the Islamic world, where the art of the stained-glass window originated, it was the practice to set the individual pieces of stained glass in a frame made of hardened stucco. The use of lead mouldings as settings seems to have originated in the Latin West; and it was this that for the first time made it possible for pieces of stained glass to be assembled, not merely in the form of ornamentation, but in the form of pictures. The monk Theophilus wrote in the twelfth century as follows:

> If you wish to assemble a stained-glass window, first of all obtain a smooth wooden board on which you can measure twice over the surface of the window concerned. Take some chalk, scrape it into the whole board with a knife, sprinkle water over it, and rub it thoroughly with a cloth. When it is dry, mark the length and breadth of the window on the board with lead or zinc, using a ruler and a compass, and, if you wish a border, trace it also in the desired size and design. Once that is done, sketch out the pictures, firstly with lead or zinc and then with red or black paint; the lines must be carefully traced for, when later you stain the glass, it is necessary to join on the board the lights and the darks. When you decide on the colours for the various garments and other items in the picture, mark the position of each colour with a letter. Then mix powdered chalk and water in a leaden vessel, and make two or three fine brushes of hair, either from the tail of a marten, a squirrel, or a cat, or from the mane of a donkey. Take a piece of glass, larger than the area into which it is to go, place it on this area and, with the chalk, mark on the glass all the designs which you see on the board underneath it.[57]

The designs painted on the pieces of glass had then to be burnt in, the pieces of glass trimmed, and all the pieces assembled on the board, in accordance with the overall design, by means of lead mouldings.

For constructional reasons, large windows were divided into a number of sections of more or less equal size. Because of this, their overall form retained something of the geometrical character of the original stained-glass windows that were made in a stucco frame. Even this the medieval artist was able to use to his advantage, by balancing motifs that corresponded to one another (from the Old and New Testaments, for example) in counterpoised panels.

The form most beloved of the Gothic masters was the rose window, for it combines in itself geometrical symbolism and the symbolism of light; it is the very quintessence of the Gothic style.

While small rose windows fill the gables of all the pairs of windows in the side walls of Chartres cathedral, three large rose windows, direct expressions of the cosmic wheel, shine like suns in the west, south and north (i.e., on the west front, and on the south and north ends of the transept). Their pictorial

On the two following pages
The rose windows of the south and north transepts of Chartres cathedral, representing the majesty of Christ and the beauty of the Blessed Virgin. The colours of the rose window on the south are not only brighter and more glowing in themselves; when the sun shines through them, they sparkle. The rose window on the north contains more blue, corresponding symbolically to the nature of the Virgin. Also, since the window faces north, it receives much less light. The south rose window, in its frontal aspect, is slightly obscured by the arm of an arch. In the centre is Christ; around him are choirs of angels and the twenty-four elders of the Apocalypse. In the windows beneath are the four Evangelists standing above the four greatest Prophets, and in the midst of them are the Virgin and Child.
In the centre of the north rose window is the enthroned Virgin with the Christ Child. Around them hover angels and the doves of the Holy Spirit. Further out, and round about them, are the kings of Judah. In the windows beneath, St. Anne is portrayed in the midst of the four priestly predecessors of Christ: Melchisedek, David, Solomon, and Aaron. St. Anne carries the child Mary and, as a sceptre, the flowering branch of Jesse.

SANCTA ANNA

dispositions correspond to the three principal meanings contained in the universal symbolism of the world-wheel.

The western rose window portrays the Last Judgement; in the centre Christ sits enthroned, surrounded by Archangels and the four beasts of the Apocalypse; He judges the resurrected, who move inwards to Him, and commits them either to the jaws of hell or the bosom of Abraham. In its perpetual rotation, the world-wheel represents the wheel of time: of becoming and passing away; its hub, however, which does not move, represents Eternity, as well as the Eternal Truth that judges all things ephemeral.

In the southern rose window is a portrayal of Christ in Majesty. Holding a chalice in His hand, He blesses the heavenly beings that move around Him, and the twenty-four elders who praise Him with their lutes; He is the Divine Sun, and the whole window is His garland of light.

In the centre of the northern rose window, the Virgin Mary sits with the Child on her lap. She holds a sceptre of fleur-de-lis. The doves of the Holy Spirit descend towards her, seraphim and cherubim hover around her, and the kings of Judah, her forefathers, form a circle around her. Here the cosmic wheel has become a rose, a flower of purity, innocence, and nobility of soul, whose calyx opens like a wheel, to receive within itself the sun of the Holy Spirit.

St. Hildegard of Bingen calls the wheel, with its beginningless and endless rotation, a symbol both of time and eternity: 'The Divinity, in Its omniscience and Its works, is always one and in no wise divided, since It has neither beginning nor end, nor can it be grasped in Its timelessness. It resembles a circle which encloses everything.'[58]

Dante writes:

> Likewise the triumph, which ever plays
> around the point that overcame me,
> seeming enclosed by That which it encloses.

Paradiso, XXX: 10–12

St. Gregory of Nazianzus had earlier sung:

> In Thee all finds its rest, and all to Thee doth move.
> For all finds its home in Thee, who art one
> and yet art no thing amongst all things.

In his description of the heavenly choirs, Dante uses the image of the rotating wheel as well as that of the calyx of a flower:

> In the form of a pure white rose
> displayed itself to me the holy militia
> which in His blood Christ made his spouse;
>
> but the other, as she flies, sees, and sings the glory
> of Him who fills her with love,
> and of the goodness which made her such,
>
> is like a swarm of bees, which at one moment
> plunges into flowers and at another
> returns to where its toil is turned to sweetness.

Thus did she descend into the large calyx,
adorned with so many petals,
and redescended thence, where her love eternally dwells.

Paradiso, XXXI: 1–12

A rose window from Lausanne cathedral, after Villard de Honnecourt.

Liturgy and Art

THE ALTAR is for the cathedral what the heart is for the body. For, through the presence of God in the sacrifice of the mass, the cathedral changes from a lifeless heap of stone into a living organism.

All ecclesiastical art grows out of the liturgy, which vehicles the Eucharistic mystery, and, in a certain sense, renders it perceptible. In that it provides a noble framework for the spoken word, hieratic vestments for the priestly office, and chants for the canonical prayers, the liturgy turns the solemnization of the mass into a sacred theatre, and, so doing, becomes the prototype of all ecclesiastical art.

The fact that, in the Gothic period, liturgical usage, though fixed and unitary in its basic form, was not yet so in all of its branches – so that it was still as it were in a 'creative' state[59] – may possibly have been a disadvantage for the outward unity of the Church: what was fruitful, however, was the resulting awareness that the liturgy itself was a semi-divine, semi-human art, which, extending outwards from its kernel in ever-widening circles, proceeds towards the Eucharistic Meal.

To the liturgy pertain interior church space and the icon. For the Eastern Orthodox Church, the holy picture or icon belongs directly to the liturgy. For, ever since the victory of the iconodules over the iconoclasts, the icon (which represents either Christ Himself, or a saint anchored in Christ) was regarded in the Christian East as the visible witness of that which, in the sacrifice of the mass, is re-enacted invisibly. Since God took on human form, He is capable of being represented pictorially, and this pictorial representation (the icon) is a means of contemplating God. This contemplation is made possible by the visible icon which evokes the invisible prototype. For the icon to fulfil this function, it has to conform, in content and in style, to sacred tradition.

The Roman Church never accorded this quasi-sacramental meaning to the icon. It regarded the holy picture principally as a means of instruction. Nevertheless, whenever (as in the Middle Ages), doctrine was understood, not merely in its most literal and ordinary sense, but on several spiritual levels simultaneously, it was in the nature of things that ecclesiastical pictorial art should also span this same range, extending from mere representation to pure 'anagogy'.

An example of this is the row of eleven sculpted figures which, in Chartres cathedral, decorate the supporting structure of the middle door of the north portal. This row begins with the figure of Melchisedec (the 'king of Salem and the priest of the Most High God' who blessed Abraham), and it ends with Peter, the priestly successor to Christ. Between them stand Abraham, Moses, Samuel, and David, and, on the other side, Isaiah, Jeremiah, the aged Simeon, and John the Baptist. All these figures are seen here as forebears of Christ, and represent Him in His dual aspect of divine priest and divine sacrifice. They thus constitute a sort of liturgical commentary.

The Apostle Paul calls Christ 'a priest for ever after the order of Melchisedec', and this is portrayed in the sculptures in that both Melchisedec and Peter hold in their hands the chalice of the Lord's supper. The former, a mysterious and foreign-looking elder, wears a partly royal, partly sacerdotal garment, while Peter is clad in the vestments of a bishop of Rome, such as were worn by the popes at the beginning of the thirteenth century.

With Abraham, who follows immediately upon Melchisedec, there begins a new and bloody, sacrifice, which was fulfilled and consummated only by Christ: the patriarch prepares to sacrifice his son Isaac; but an angel, who is shown on his left side, prevents him from so doing, and points to the ram at the boy's feet. This biblical scene is a clear example of the fact that (as the medieval exegetes, following an ancient tradition, maintained) every image in Holy Scripture can be interpreted in several senses. William Durandus writes that, in Holy Scripture, there are four principal meanings: historical, allegorical, tropological, and anagogical. 'Historically, Jerusalem is the city in Palestine to which people went on pilgrimage; allegorically (or morally), it is the Church Militant; tropologically, it is the Christian soul; and anagogically, it is the Heavenly Jerusalem, the eternal home.'

As applied to the sacrifice of Abraham, the historical interpretation teaches how, on God's command, the sacrifical animal took the place of the human victim. One sees this again in the hands of the fourth member of the series of sculptures: Samuel, his head covered, prepares the sacrifical lamb. It appears once again in the hands of the tenth and penultimate figure, this time with the inscription, to which John the Baptist points: *Agnus Dei qui tollis peccata mundi* ('Lamb of God who bearest the sins of the world'). The sacrificial animal, which took the place of Isaac, is here portrayed as the prototype of the God-Man.

Allegorically speaking, Abraham, by offering his son, beloved over all else, to God, sacrifices himself.

Tropologically, through the intended sacrifice of Isaac, his whole posterity, Israel, is sanctified; for whatever is sacrificed to God, and received back from Him as a gift, is holy. And this leads us to the anagogical sense, which is here intended above all others: the sacrifice of the God-Man.

Between Abraham and Samuel stands Moses with the Tables of the Law and also a pillar on which there is a bronze snake, a prototype of Christ on the cross.

Samuel is followed by David, the king who suffered for his people, bearing the crown of thorns.

On the facing door support, the first figure is that of Isaiah, who points to the 'branch that grew out of the roots of Jesse' (*Isaiah*, XI:1); this branch arises from Jesse, who lies under the feet of the prophet.

Jeremiah, who comes next, bears on his breast a cross inscribed in a circle.

The aged Simeon carries in his arms the Christ Child, whom he had received on the altar. After him comes John the Baptist, and finally Peter.

With regard to these figures, Emile Mâle has very pertinently written:

> The mysterious chalice which, at the beginning of the world's history, appears in the hands of Melchisedec, is finally to be seen in the hands of St. Peter. In this way, the cycle is completed. Each of these personages is thus a kind of Christophorus, a 'bearer of Christ', and they all hand on the mysterious symbol from one generation to the next.[60]

According to the interpretation of the Medieval exegetes, which follows that of the Church Fathers, the Old Testament expresses the truths of the New Testament in a hidden manner: *Quod Moysis doctrina velat, Christi doctrina revelat* ('What Moses' teaching veils, Christ's teaching reveals'). These words were inscribed by Suger on one of the stained-glass windows of the church of Saint-Denis. According to the same interpretation, the priesthood of the Old Covenant pertains to God as Lord of the Law and the cosmic order, while the priesthood of the New Covenant is the expression and the vehicle of grace.

Innocent III, in his work *De sacro altaris mysterio*,[61] written around 1200, interprets even priestly vestments according to this point of view. Of the adornment of the Jewish high priest, he writes:

> When he was adorned in these vestments, the high priest carried on his person a symbol of the universe. The white surround can be called a symbol of the earth, for the flax of which it is made comes from the earth. The girdle, with its threads and openings, represented the ocean, which surrounds the earth. The yellow robe, by its colour, signified the air, the bells [which were attached to it] the roaring of thunder, and the [golden] pomegranates the flashing of lightning. The number four, which governed the vestments of both the high and the lower priests, referred to the four humours or the four elements. The coat of many colours represented the starry sky. The fact that its colours were interwoven with gold evoked the warmth of life that penetrates everything. The two onyx stones [which were attached to the shoulders of the coat] evoked the sun and the moon or the two heavenly hemispheres, just as the twelve precious stones of the breastplate recalled the twelve signs of the zodiac. It was known as 'the plumb-line of judgement', since it

Figures on the pillar on the right of the right-hand entrance of the south doorway: Saints Martin, Hieronymus, Gregory, and Avitus.

was placed in the middle, and since everything that links the earthly with the heavenly is arranged in proper order. The order of earthly things – such as winter/spring/summer/autumn or cold/dryness/heat/moisture – is governed by the rotation of the heavens. The interconnection of the seasons, sensible qualities, elements, and humours,[62] was indicated by the rings, chains, and clasps [which bound the breastplate to the onyx stones on the shoulders]. The headpiece signified the visible heavens, and the gold plate covering it the all-governing Divinity. The justness of this interpretation is confirmed in the Book of Wisdom, in which it is written: 'In his long robe was the whole globe, the great deeds of the forefathers were engraved on four rows of stone, and Thy glory was written on his headband.'

The vestments of the priest of the Gospels, on the other hand, mean something else in their relationship to the head and limbs.

The *amictus*, with which the priest covers his head, corresponds to the cloud mentioned in the Apocalypse where it is said that a mighty angel of the Lord descended swathed in a cloud.

The alb, a garment of linen contrasting with the coat of skins with which Adam clothed himself after his sin, signifies new life . . . of which the Apostle says: 'Take off the old man and all his actions, and put on the new man created in the image of God'. For at the Transfiguration 'the Lord's face shone like the sun, and his raiment was white as snow. . . .'

By means of the golden girdle, Christ's perfect love is signified . . . the Apostle says: 'As I turned, I saw a man like the Son of Man, girded beneath the breast with a golden girdle.'

The stole, known also as the prayer-cloth, is placed by the priest around his neck, to show that he has accepted the yoke of the Lord. . . .

The tunic signifies the heavenly teaching of Christ. It was prefigured by the robe which the soldiers were unwilling to divide because it was seamless. . . .

Over the tunic, the senior priest throws the dalmatic which, in its width, represents the mercy of Christ. . . .

The Bishop's gloves indicate prudence. . . .

The chasuble signifies love, for 'love covers a multitude of sins' . . . Love is also the wedding garment of which the King speaks in the Gospel: 'Friend, how camest thou in hither not having a wedding garment?' . . .

The mitre of the senior priest indicates knowledge of the two Testaments, these being symbolized by the two peaks. . . .

The [bishop's] ring is the emblem of faithfulness. . . .

The [bishop's] staff means pastoral guidance. . . .

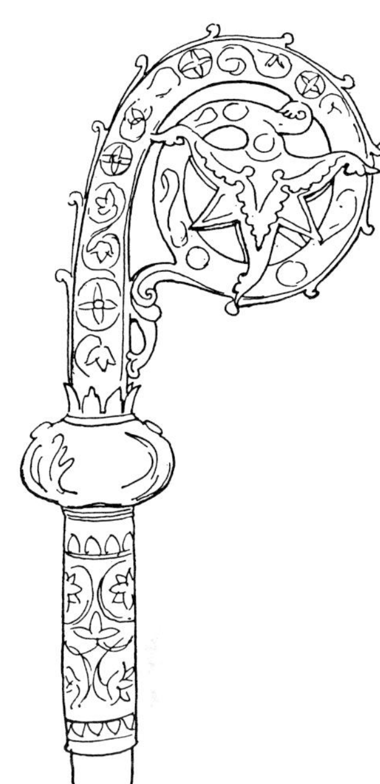

The staff (thirteenth century) of Pierre de Charny, Archbishop of Sens. The crook, decorated with coloured enamels, ends in a blossom, like the blossoming rod of Aaron.

❨

The contemplative faculty which sees a spiritual imagery in the hieratic forms of the liturgy inevitably calls for an art for which the most perfect form is the hieratic. An example of this are the eleven wall-statues spoken of above. They are the earliest of all the groups of figures which decorate the northern and southern doorways (at either end of the transept) of Chartres cathedral and which together constitute a single great thematic exposition which was planned as such from the beginning, but which only gradually came into being between the beginning and the middle of the thirteenth century.

Compared with the statues of the Royal Door, these eleven 'bearers of Christ' may already be considered to be almost naturalistic. They no longer possess the form—completely bound to the building, yet spiritually radiant—of the kings and patriarchs of the early Gothic doorway, though they do remain attached to the wall in the form of a sort of relief. One has the impression that the sculptor first drew the outlines of each figure on the surface of a rectangular block of stone, and then hewed out the figure in depth. For this very reason, they seem more awkward than most of the late Gothic statues, which, as if sculpted after a free-standing model, seem to move outwards from their own axis. But the great advantage of the statues done before 1220, to which the Apostles on the surrounds of the central door of the south portal also belong, lies in the fact that their features do not yet depart from the broadly conceived form of a traditional type. On looking at them, one never asks whether this or that prophet or saint really looked like this; it is sufficient that his appearance should, in general terms, look probable. In the case of the later statues, on the other hand, one involuntarily exclaims: 'The Virgin Mary could never have looked like this! The Prophet Solomon could never have had a face like that!' The more the artist succeeds in creating the impression of a living human being, and in capturing the expression of a fleeting moment (thus deliberately departing from a universal prototype), the less probable it is that his image is truly veridical, and the more disturbingly does his own individualized conception obtrude in the believer's imagination—an imagination nourished by Holy Scripture.

Only occasionally does an outstanding artist, as the fruit of his own spiritual maturity, succeed in convincingly creating a saint's likeness down to the minutest physical details, as if these had been observed from life. This applies, for example, in the case of the master who created the statues of Saints Martin, Hieronymus and Gregory on the right-hand wall of the right-hand door of the south portal. But even in this case, the hieratic bearing and the markedly aristocratic sensibility of his time protected him from arbitrariness. A generation later, art, whenever it sought to portray human figures naturalistically, was unable any longer to distance itself from the prevailing semi-courtly, semi-bourgeois mentality, as can be seen, admittedly in a still gentle and charming manner, in the much admired statue of St. Modesta on a pillar in the north atrium.

The statue of the teaching Saviour, that stands on the central doorpost of the south portal between the two groups of Apostles ranged on either side, indicates the extreme permissible limit of the tendency that ultimately leads to human nearness, psychological representation, and finally naturalism: much of the mystery that makes the *Majestas Domini* of the Royal Door so otherworldly and so radiant, is here already lost. The statue on the south portal of the teaching and blessing Christ gives above all the impression of a noble, harmonious, and wise human being. And yet, because the artist eschewed all sentimentalism, its appearance is still much more spiritual than the majority of the later statues of Christ. The gentle motionlessness of the expression alone leaves a door open to the ineffable. Also, it should not be forgotten that the former practice of painting the statue—the darker colour of the hair (as compared with the face), the emphasizing of the eyes, and the golden sheen of the halo—must have made the sculpted countenance of Christ look like an icon.

Figures on the left-hand pillar of the central entrance of the north doorway: Melchisedek with chalice and censer, Abraham with Isaac bound ready for sacrifice, Moses with the tables of the law and the brass snake in the form of a dragon, Samuel with the sacrificial lamb, and David.

The statues of the north portal all relate to the Old Covenant and the preparation for the coming of Christ, while those of the south portal all relate to the New Covenant. The statues on the portals thus observe the same liturgical disposition as do the respective stained-glass windows.

The north and south portals each have three entrances, so that the arrangement of the statues on them is tripartite, rather like the altar triptychs of later times. The main statues are always positioned around the central entrance: on the central entrance of the north portal, in two groups, are the eleven 'bearers of Christ' of whom we have already spoken, and between them, on the pillar supporting

See drawing on pages 122–125.

the lintel, is the statue of St. Anne with the infant Mary in her arms. The former carry the tokens of the Divine Word, while the latter carries her who is to be the vessel of its Incarnation. The dominant position of St. Anne may be explained by the fact that Chartres cathedral possessed one of her relics. The glory of the Virgin Mary herself fills the whole of the central tympanum: following *The Golden Legend*, it is depicted how she died in the presence of the Apostles, how the angel lifted up her body from the grave, and how she was crowned by Christ in Heaven. It is an appropriately inward glorification of the Queen of Heaven, such as was first seen in the cathedral at Senlis and was to become so dear to the people of the thirteenth century, that it was subsequently portrayed hundreds of times.

The statues on the wall supports of the right-hand entrance are devoted to the human prefigurations of Jesus and Mary: King Solomon and the Queen of Sheba, seen here talking together, symbolize Christ and His Church. Near them, sitting on a she-ass, is Balaam, who prophesied the birth of the Saviour. Opposite, on the other wall support, are Joseph and Judith, and next to them is the prophet Jesus Sirach. On the right-hand tympanum, the Judgement of Solomon and the tribulations of Job are represented.

On the wall supports of the left-hand (or eastern-most) entrance of the north portal, two group compositions stand facing one another: the Annunciation (the Archangel Gabriel and the Virgin Mary) and the Visitation (the Virgin Mary at the house of St. Elizabeth); these are accompanied by the prophets Daniel and Isaiah, who prophesied the coming of the Messiah. The figures of Leah and Rachel, representing respectively the active and the contemplative life, were destroyed at the time of the French Revolution, as were also the statues of Church and Synagogue. The story of Christ's birth is continued in the left-hand tympanum, where the Nativity, the Annunciation to the shepherds, the Dream of the Magi, and the Adoration of the Magi are represented.

Around the central entrance of the south portal are the twelve apostles; around the left-hand entrance, the martyrs; and around the right-hand entrance, the confessors. All of these relate to the teaching Christ, who stands on the door pillar of the central entrance. On the lower part of the central tympanum is a representation of the Last Judgement. This seems to contradict the otherwise respected liturgical order, according to which the Last Judgement would be represented in the west, opposite the choir. But here the Last Judgement is like a prolongation of the *Majestas* that occupies the upper part of the tympanum; it is an expression of Divine victory and glory. Indeed the figure of Christ in Majesty, together with the Blessed Virgin and St. John the Evangelist, form a kind of deësis, which angels approach bearing the instruments of the Passion. The cathedral of Chartres believed that it possessed relics of these instruments.

The martyrs on the wall supports of the left-hand door are Stephen, Clement and Laurence, who are accompanied by the holy warrior Theodore, then by three priests Vincent, Dionysius and Piat, and finally by the holy warrior St. George. The statues of the two knights, Theodore and George, are evidently of later construction than the other statues; they give the appearance of being true to life, and yet they are typical of their kind, because in them the knightly ideal of their time finds direct expression. The left-hand tympanum portrays the history of the protomartyr Stephen.

The martyrs are 'witnesses' to Christ through their sacrificial death, which unites them to him; the confessors witness Christ in truth. The confessors are represented, on one wall of the left-hand door, by Saints Nicholas, Ambrose, and

Statue of the preaching Christ on the doorpost of the central entrance of the south doorway. Christ is standing on a lion and a dragon, symbols of death and sin. Above his head is the heavenly city with twelve towers. Underneath (not shown here), the works of charity, to which Christ's sermon refers, are represented.

Leo (all bishops), and St. Laumer (who came from the diocese), and, on the opposite wall, by Saints Martin, Jerome and Gregory, and the local Saint Avitus. Saints Martin and Nicholas were miracle workers, Saints Jerome and Ambrose were doctors of the Church, and Saints Leo and Gregory were Popes. In the tympanum above the left-hand door the lives of Saints Nicholas and Martin are portrayed.

Both doorways of the transept are overshadowed by vaulted porches, on whose pillars stand statues of prophets and Old-Testament kings and saints, and whose arches are decorated by garlands of small figures or scenes in relief. These represent the various realms of nature and of the soul. Amongst other things, there are representations of the Six Days of Creation, the Four Rivers of Paradise, the signs of the Zodiac, the months, and the seasons; allegorical figures represent the virtues and vices, the active and contemplative lives, the gifts of the Holy Spirit, and the delights of the Elect.

This presentation of a spiritual psychology is typical of the thirteenth century: one might say that it was then that men began to think psychologically. But it was not psychology in the modern sense of the word that was practised in those days, for all the movements of the soul were seen against the background of a spiritual certainty that transcended the merely psychic. For this very reason, both the lights and shadows of the soul stood out in all their clarity.

These statues correspond perfectly to the meaning of a porch, which constitutes the entry into a sanctuary.

Between its three gables, and on the side of the eaves, the south portal is surmounted by a sort of crown of arcades, in which stand the statues of the kings of Judah. These are flanked by two unfinished towers. With these towers, and the large rose window above, the south portal was probably intended to form the new and definitive façade of the church, after the older west front had been outshone by the striking west front of the cathedral of Laon, with its deep porches, immense window niches, and open arcades. On the upward-striving walls of the transept and the lower parts of the two towers, wall pillars fine as harp strings rise up: an expressive device that was to reach its full development on the luminous and apparently weightless façade of the cathedral of Strasbourg.

It is noteworthy that all the sculptural decoration is concentrated on the portals: it proliferates in the porches and, on the doors themselves, with their wall-supports, tympanums and pillars, it reaches its dramatic highpoint. Then suddenly, when one goes through the door into the church itself, all sculpture disappears; even the late-Gothic sculpture which surrounds the choir, and which was not part of the original plan for the cathedral, at first escapes the eye; it rises above the simple and undecorated architectural forms towards the ethereal stained-glass windows, seemingly made of light.

Symbolically speaking, the door that leads into the sanctuary represents the passage from one world to another, from earthly existence to the Kingdom of God; outside, the myriad of physical objects remains, while inside reigns the splendour of light.

Schematic representation of the tripartite north doorway of Chartres cathedral. The figures on the inner jambs are partially obstructed by the pillars and statues of the porches.

South façade of Chartres cathedral—view across roof-tops.

The door, which architecturally is space-occupying, becomes, as one goes through it, a moment of transition that may be likened to death, judgement, and rebirth. Contrariwise, the whole sacred edifice, whose basic form depends on the orientation deriving from the movements of the heavens, is once again transmuted, by the liturgical acts that take place on the altar and radiate from it, into a temporal succession.

South façade of Chartres cathedral: only the lower parts of the two towers which were intended to frame the southern end of the transept were completed.

The so-called 'draft B' for the west front of Strasbourg Cathedral, drawn around 1270. The body of the building is here completely dissolved in a web of lines, which seem to pertain more to the nature of light than to that of stone.

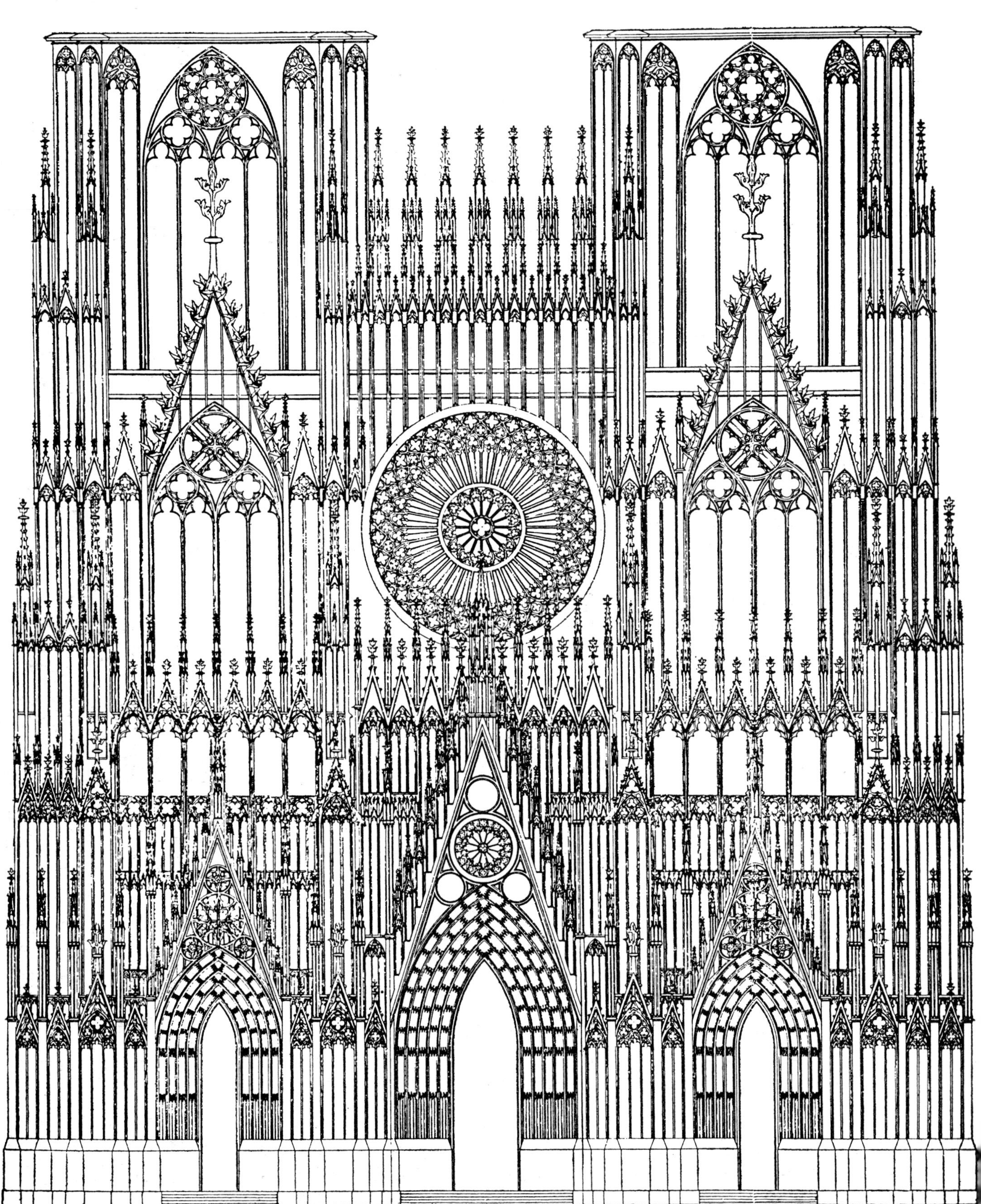

Epilogue: The Temple of the Holy Grail

THE groundplans of the Gothic cathedrals, from Chartres to Beauvais, clearly indicate the intention to gather around a centre the space created by luminous baldachins. This can never succeed entirely, for the liturgical centre of the space cannot coincide with the geometrical centre, so that the shape of the church always retains something of the nature of a 'way' leading towards the altar. However, in a poem stemming from chivalric mysticism, 'Titurel' by Albrecht von Scharffenberg, the ideal of concentric construction in the Gothic form is described as the Temple of the Grail.[63] Albrecht composed his work in German around 1270, but, like his predecessor Wolfram von Eschenbach, he did so from French sources, so that one may justifiably link it with the Gothic construction then emanating from France. It would nevertheless be wrong to see in the poetic description of the Temple of the Grail the reflection, or the basis, of a true architecture; its value lies in clearly expressing a certain aspect of the symbolic imagination which in the church architecture of the time was only hinted at.

The Temple of the Grail is round, for the Grail represents not only the sacred centre of the building but also the secret centre of the world.

The Grail is the symbol of the heart as vessel of Divine Knowledge. In terms of its origin, this symbol is pre-Christian, having passed over to the Christian Middle Ages from the Celtic tradition. When Chrétien de Troyes describes the Grail as the chalice in which Joseph of Arimathaea caught and preserved the blood flowing from the wounds of Christ, this is a later, but entirely meaningful explanation of a primordial symbol; the symbol thereby assumes the significance of the eucharistic chalice, while at the same time remaining something else.

In Albrecht's poem, Titurel says:

None can fully interpret the symbolic language of the Grail,
Neither lips nor tongue. Mark well, for Christians worthy of the name,
I caused the Temple to be built, according to right science, that they,
As faithful of the Temple, might therein see true signs of God.

In the image of Jerusalem in Holy Paradise
Stands our Temple of the Grail, and yet it resembles
This prototype as much as the brightness of a piece of burning straw
Illumines the world around it in place of the sun.

Man – in his pure state – is like the Temple; he needs beauty,
For in beauty God wills to unite Himself with the human soul,
As with the guest within His house.
Arise, O noble human heart, and make thy body great in noble virtue!

Albrecht relates how King Titurel built the Temple on the top of a mountain that towered above all others, and which from the ground up was composed of a single onyx, which had been overgrown with grass and vegetation. This is nothing other than the legendary world mountain, which the Arabs call *Qâf*, the Persians

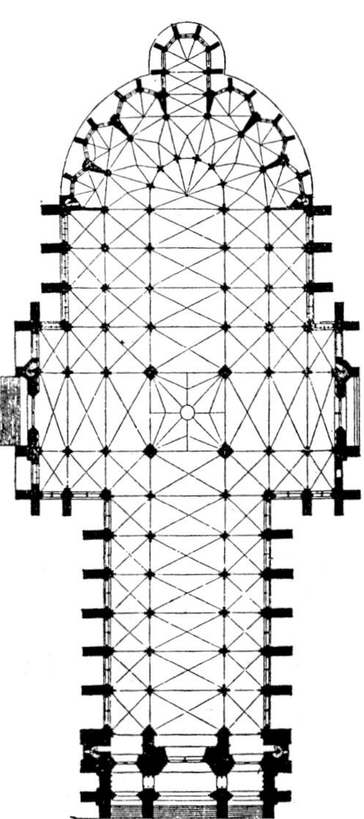

Groundplan of Amiens cathedral. As in the case of Chartres, the wide space of the crossing forms the optical centre of the whole building.

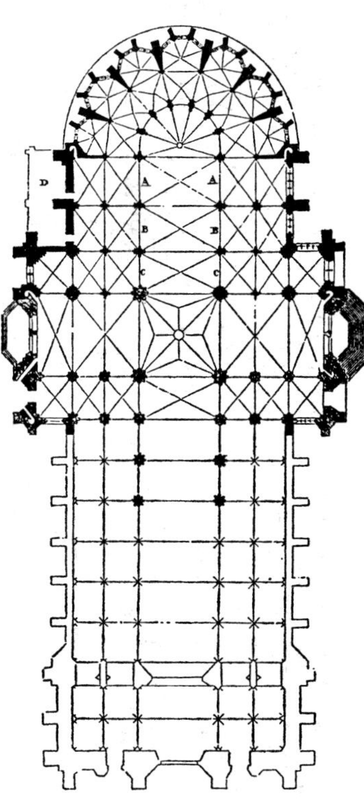

Groundplan of Beauvais cathedral. The parts sketched only in outline were in the original plan but were never realized.

Alborj, and the Indians *Meru*. It corresponds to the axis around which the heavens turn, and is thus the symbol of immutable Spirit, the true centre of the universe.

The King, Albrecht goes on, commanded that the surface of the onyx, which was more than six hundred feet wide and formed the summit of the mountain, be uncovered and polished until it shone like the moon. And immediately there appeared upon it, thanks to the secret power of the Grail, the plan for the temple with all its measurements. The mirror-flat surface of the onyx mountain signifies the readiness of the spirit or intellect to receive divine inspiration. This recalls the building of the Temple at Jerusalem, whose plan and dimensions were revealed to David in a vision.

> The foundations, he found them already dug,
> In the form of a circle, like a rotunda.
> In breadth and depth, one could count seventy-two choirs,
> Everywhere around, and every one outstanding.

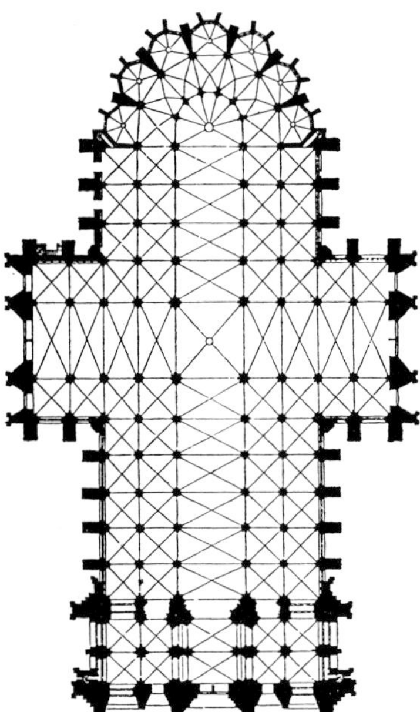

The groundplan of Cologne cathedral clearly manifests the ideal of universal space.

The principal choir, which faces east, is twice as wide as the others. It is dedicated to the Holy Ghost, Patron of the Temple. Nearby, there is a choir dedicated to the Blessed Virgin, and another dedicated to St. John the Evangelist. In the middle of the circular building, as a smaller and richly decorated temple, stands the sanctuary of the Grail.

The rotunda has three doors, facing south, west, and north. In the south, there are also the palace and the dormitory of the Knights Templar, who guard the Temple.

The arches of the edifice rest on bronze pillars; these pier arches stretch from pillar to pillar, and above them is the vaulting.

A central tower rises above the sanctuary, and round about stands a garland of octagonal bell towers, each one of them covering two choirs. Each of these bell towers has six stories, and in each wall of the octagonal stories are three windows. These numbers clearly refer to the cyclical significance of the building: the 72 choirs, the 36 towers, the six-times 24 windows in each tower; all of them are multiples of 12. When one takes into consideration that in each of the choirs (as it is further related) 10 incense burners are burning, one obtains, by multiplication, the figure 25,920, which expresses in terms of years the complete precession of the equinoxes. This is the great cosmic measure, to which the Apocalyptic description of the Heavenly Jerusalem also refers; like the latter, the Temple of the Grail is an image of the cosmos. In particular, the number of windows in each tower, namely 144, corresponds to the height of the walls of the Heavenly City.

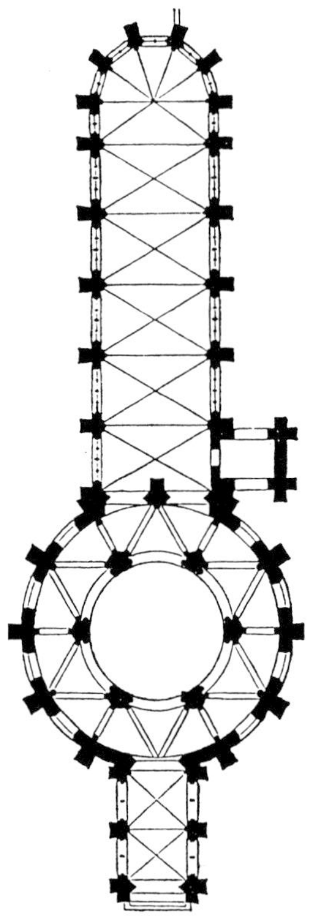

The sanctuary of the Knights-Templar in Paris (first half of twelfth century), the so-called 'Temple', with its twelve-part rotunda; after Viollet-le-Duc.

Moreover, the figures 6, 8, 36, and 72, which were mentioned above, also occur in the composition of medieval imperial crowns; this is not surprising, as the crown likewise represents the circumference of the heavens or the Heavenly City.[64]

The vaulting of the Temple of the Grail is covered with pure sapphire, blue as cornflower, and shining carbuncles are scattered over it like stars. There are also a golden sun and a silver-white moon; these move in their orbits, propelled by an invisible clock.

Such mechanisms occur several times in 'Titurel'; they did not make the same bizarrely artificial impression on the medieval reader as they do on us; medieval man could still see the cosmic dimension in mechanical laws, and, in the wheels of a clock, a reflection of the universal order. With such images, Albrecht von Scharffenberg is referring, in an intentionally playful way, to the cosmic significance of the Temple of the Grail.

Thus, on the floor of the Temple, the mechanically driven image of the world-sea can be seen. All manner of figures of fish and other sea creatures have been carved out of the onyx and left to slide on the ground, and over them was a covering of crystal.

Bellows, blowing air under the crystal covering from outside, caused the figures to move, *as if they were alive in the waves*:

> The appearance of the crystal covering made the eyes believe
> That a sea moved underneath, which yet was covered with 'ice'
> That one could see through; and what a tumult
> Of fish, animals, and sea wonders was there.

The image of the world-sea (moved by the four winds and teeming with monsters), which can be seen on some medieval miniatures, is here transposed into a mechanical plaything. That precisely the floor of the Temple should represent the ocean may seem to be in contradiction with its position on the summit of a mountain; strictly speaking, the world-sea should surround its base. But the symbolic poem blithely passes over such contradictions. For it, what is important is that the edifice, whose roof corresponds to Heaven, should rest, in its depths, on the world-sea. There are pre-Christian temples which, with their ceiling paintings and floor mosaics, exemplify this same vision of things.[65] Also, some Asian temples and sacred palaces, like the Potala at Lhasa, are conceived as a holy mountain surrounded by water, or completely resting on it; the water or the world-sea is like the stuff of all ephemeral appearances, above which the immutable temple of the Spirit rises.

In keeping with this, the temple of the Grail has no crypt:

> Were there crypts there? May God forbid
> That, in crypts in the earth, purity should mingle with falsehood;
> For this might easily happen. The Christian faith,
> And the Christian's duty, must be proclaimed in the light of day!

This point of view, it has been said, is an example of the typically Gothic passion for light. This opinion is also supported by the fact that the Temple of the Grail was illumined by coloured windows:

> They were not fitted with windows of ash-grey glass.
> They were luminous crystals; low cost was dismissed from thence.
> Beryls and crystals took the place of glass.

Since, however, the light which transpierced the crystals was too strong for the eyes, they were coated with ground precious stones: sapphire, emerald, amethyst, topaz, hyacinth, sardonyx, ruby, cornelian, chrysoprase, and many others. These precious stones do not only supply many colours, they also possess the property of awakening certain virtues which are described in another part of the poem. For, in a certain way, each precious stone not only gathers within itself an animic or psychic quality, but is also the focus of a certain spiritual light, which it has the capacity to radiate or transmit. It is said of the sapphire, for example, that, rightly handled, it has the power to free the soul from sin, in that it can help it, like the water that flows towards the mountains, to find its way back to God.

Inside, the choirs are divided by precious partitions, each of which has two doors. Their walls are decorated with spiral pillars, which are connected by arches. Above them rise trees of gold, filled with birds. On all the arches golden vines are entwined; they meet one another above and fall down over the stools below. They provide shade from the brilliance of the emerald-covered walls.

> The foliage is so thick that, whenever there is a breath of air,
> One could, without fear, hear it tinkle in a sweet way,
> As if a thousand falcons gathered in a flock,
> And golden bells tinkled on them.

A rather curious metallic symbol for the Garden of Paradise! Of similar nature is an organ, in the shape of a red-gold tree, above the west entrance, full of singing birds, each of which sings high or low, 'depending on the key'.

> Four angels on the branches, two on each edge,
> Stood faultless, each with a golden horn in his hand,
> Which they blew with a great sound,
> And waved, with their other hand, to say: awaken, all ye dead!

Notes

1 *The Construction of the Gothic Cathedrals: A Study of Medieval Vault Erection*, Oxford University Press, 1961.

2 Perennial Books, Bedfont, Middlesex, 1967.

3 Lothar Kitscheld, *Die frühchristliche Basilika als Darstellung des himmlischen Jerusalem*, Munich 1939.

4 See Julius Schwabe, *Archetyp und Tierkreis*, Basel 1951.

5 A. Dupont-Sommer, 'Une Hymne syriaque sur la Cathédrale d'Edesse', in *Cahiers Archéologiques*, II, 1947.

6 See O. Wulff, 'Das Raumerlebnis des Naos in der Ekphrasis', *Byzantinische Zeitschrift*, volume 30, 1929/30.

7 *Ibid.*

8 *Ibid.*

9 Honorius Augustodunensis: *Gemmae animae; sacramentarium*, Patrologia Latina Migne, CLXXII.

10 Guillaume Durand de Mende: *Rationale divinorum officiorum*, French translation by Charles Barthélemy, Paris 1854.

11 Titus Burckhardt, *Sacred Art in East and West*, Chapter I, 'The Genesis of the Hindu Temple'.

12 See Vitruvius, Book I, chapter VI; Alhard von Drach, *Das Hüttengeheimnis vom gerechten steinmetzen-Grund*, Marburg 1897; Stella Kramrisch, *The Hindu Temple*, University of Calcutta, 1946; Rudolf Moessel, *Die Proportion in Antike und Mittelalter*, Munich 1926.

13 Louis IX (1214–70), King of France from 1226 to 1270.

14 Suger, *Vie de Louis VI le Gros*, translated by H. Waquet, Paris 1929.

15 Suger, *op. cit.*

16 Suger, *op. cit.*

17 Dionysius Areopagita, *The Celestial Hierarchy*.

18 Dionysius Areopagita, *The Divine Names*.

19 Dionysius Areopagita, *The Celestial Hierarchy*.

20 L. Delisle, 'Traductions de textes faites par des religieux de Saint-Denis au XIIe siècle', *Journal des Savants*, Paris 1900.

21 Abbot Suger, *On the Abbey Church of St. Denis*, translated and edited by Erwin Panofsky, Princeton 1946. See also: E. Gall, *Die gotische Baukunst in Frankreich und Deutschland*, volume 1, Leipzig 1925.

22 See: St. Bernard, *Oeuvres mystiques*, translated by Albert Béguin, Paris 1953.

23 Abbot Suger, *op. cit.*

24 *Ibid.*

25 See: Victor Mortet and Paul Deschamps, *Recueil de textes relatifs à l'histoire de l'Architecture*, p. 81 *et seq.*

26 See: Hugo Lämmer, *Caelestis urbs Hierusalem*, Freiburg 1866.

27 *Chronique de Robert de Torigny*, published by Léopold Delisle (Société de l'histoire de France), volume 1, I. 1872.

28 See: M. J. Bulteau, *Monographie de la Cathédrale de Chartres*, 2nd edition, Chartres, 1887–92, 3 volumes.

29 V. Mortet and P. Deschamps, *op. cit.*

30 M. J. Bulteau, *op. cit.*

31 V. Mortet and P. Deschamps, *op. cit.*

32 See: Emile Male, *L'Art religieux du XIIIe siècle en France*, Paris 1931, p. 188 *et seq.*

33 St. Albert the Great, Collection *Les Maitres de la Spiritualité chrétienne*, Mariale, CLXII, 13–14, translated by Albert Carreau, Paris 1942.

34 René Guénon, *Fundamental Symbols*, chapter 37, 'The Solstitial Gate', Quinta Essentia, Cambridge 1995.

35 Thierry of Chartres: *Handbook of the Seven Liberal Arts*, quoted in *Das Königsportal von Chartres* by Wolfgang Schöne, Reclam, Stuttgart, 1961.

36 A. M. S. Boethius, *De Arithmetica libri duo.*

37 J. M. Parent: *La doctrine de la création dans l'École de Chartres*, Paris 1938 (Thierry: *Librum hunc*).

38 William of Conques: *Philosophia mundi. Patrologia latina* Migne, CLXXII, 39–115.

39 See: Régine Pernoud, *Lumière du Moyen Age*, Paris, 1944.

40 See: M. J. Bulteau, *op. cit.*

41 *Miracula Beatae Mariae Virginis in Cartonensi ecclesia facta*, edited by A. Thomas, Bibliothèque de l'École de Chartres, XVII, 1881.

42 See: M. J. Bulteau, *op. cit.*

43 *Miracula Beatae Mariae Virginis in Cartonensi ecclesia facta*, edited by A. Thomas, Bibliothèque de l'École de Chartres, XVII, 1881.

44 John Fitchen, *op. cit.*.

45 Stella Kramrisch, *op. cit.*

46 W. Überwasser: *Nach rechtem Mass: Jahrbuch der preussischen Kunstsammlungen*, 56, 1935.

47 Otto von Simson, *The Gothic Cathedral: Origins of Gothic Architecture and the Medieval Concept of Order*, Bollingen Series, XLVIII, New York, 1956.

48 Otto von Simson, *op. cit.*

49 Otto von Simson, *op. cit.*

50 Scotus Eriugena, *Periphyseon.*

51 J. M. Parent, *La Doctrine de la création dans l'École de Chartres*, Paris 1938 (Thierry, *Librum hunc*).

52 P. Duhem, *Les Origines de la statique*, Paris 1905.

53 J. S. Ackerman, '*Ars sine scientiâ nihil est*: the Gothic Theory of Architecture at the Cathedral of Milan', *Art Bulletin*, XXXI, 1949.

54 C. Alhard von Drach, *Das Hüttengeheimnis vom gerechten Steinmetzen-Grund*, Marburg, 1897.

55 Durandus and Honorius Augustodunensis. See *Symbolik des Kirchengebäudes* by Josef Sauer.

56 Ulrich Engelberti of Strasbourg, *De pulchro*. See Ananda K. Coomaraswamy, 'The Medieval Theory of Beauty' in *Selected Papers 1: Traditional Art and Symbolism* (p. 194), edited by Roger Lipsey, Bollingen Series LXXXIX, New York, 1977.

57 Theophilus Presbiter: *Schema diversarum artium*; in *Quellenschriften zur Kunstgeschichte*, volume VII.

58 St. Hildegard of Bingen: *De Operatione Dei.*

59 J. A. Jungman: *Missarium Solemnia, Collection Théologie*, studies published by the Faculty of Theology of the Society of Jesus of Lyon-Fourvière, Paris 1956.

60 Emile Mâle, *op. cit.*

61 Innocence III: *De sacro altaris mysterio*, Patrologia Latina, Migne CCXVII.

62 See page 24 of this book.

63 *Der jüngere Titurel*, edited by K. A. Hahn, Quedlinburg and Leipzig 1842. See also Blanca Röthlisberger, *Die Architectur des Gralstempels im jüngeren Titurel* (Series *Sprache und Dichtung*, Volume 18), Bern 1917.

64 Borsig-Schramm, *Die Kaiserinsignien.*

65 K. Lehmann, 'The Dome of Heaven', *Art Bulletin*, 27 (1945).

Index

Acknowledgements

The publisher's gratitude is extended to those who, in their several ways, have made this book possible. To Mme Edith Burckhardt for graciously permitting this English translation. To William Stoddart for so painstakingly preparing the translation. To Keith Critchlow for his Foreword and generosity in giving advice and guidance. To Michael Pollack, Martin Lings and Clive Hicks for their commitment to the welfare of the project. To Stephen Overy and Arthur Versluis for reading the proofs. To Donna Thin and Emma Clark for picture research. To Sonia Halliday, Laura Lushington and Clive Hicks for their help in supplying photographs and to Alan Goodfellow for his forbearance in the pursuit of excellence. The translator specially wishes to thank Mr Nicholas Stone of Stuttgart and Sri Keshavram Iengar of Mysore for their professional assistance in the translation of the many architectural technical terms which occur in the text.

Picture credits are as follows: pages 18, 55, 62, 90, 106, 107, 110, 111, 116, 121 are copyright Sonia Halliday and Laura Lushington. Pages 45, 50, 59, 66, 68, 73, 74, 77, 86, 87, 95, 119, 124 are copyright Clive Hicks. Page 23 Scala Art Resource, New York; page 30 The Pierpoint Morgan Library, New York, M.644, f222v; page 26 The National Gallery, London. The drawings from John Fitchen's *The Construction of Gothic Cathedrals* are reproduced, copyright, by kind permission of the University of Chicago Press. The many line drawings that appear throughout the book are taken from the original German edition and are by the author. Grateful acknowledgement is also made to the Matheson Trust for a grant towards the cost of production and to the Marc Fitch Fund for a grant towards the cost of illustrations.